D1278336

# THE BESIEGED DESERT

# THE BESIEGED DESERT

## WAR, DROUGHT, POACHING IN THE NAMIB DESERT
### Mitch Reardon

COLLINS

William Collins Sons and Co Ltd
London · Glasgow · Sydney · Auckland · Toronto · Johannesburg

Previous page: *Desert elephants crossing the basalt laval plains*

First published in Great Britain 1986
© Mitch Reardon
ISBN 0 00 219040 6
Typeset by Servis Filmsetting Ltd, Manchester
Colour originated by Culver Graphics Ltd., High Wycombe
Printed and bound by Toppan Printing Co. Ltd., Singapore

# Contents

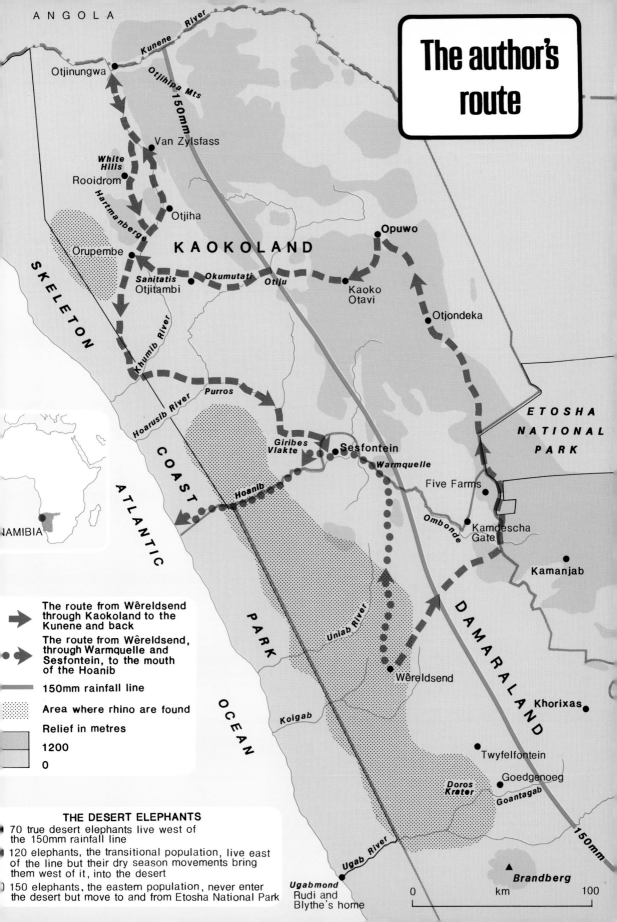

ANGOLA

Kunene River

Otjinungwa

Otjihipa Mts
150mm

Van Zylsfass

*White Hills*
Rooidrom

*Hartmanberge*

Otjiha

Orupembe

KAOKOLAND

*Sanitatis*
Otjitambi  *Okumutati*  *Otjiu*

Kaoko Otavi

Opuwo

Otjondeka

SKELETON

*Khumib River*

*Hoarusib River*  *Purros*

*Giribes Vlakte*  Sesfontein

*Warmquelle*

COAST

*Hoanib*

Five Farms

*Ombonde*  Kamdescha Gate

ETOSHA NATIONAL PARK

ATLANTIC

NAMIBIA

Kamanjab

PARK

*Uniab River*

Wêreldsend

DAMARALAND

Khorixas

OCEAN

*Koigab*

*Twyfelfontein*

*Goedgenoeg*

*Doros Krater*  *Goantagab*

# The author's route

The route from Wêreldsend through Kaokoland to the Kunene and back

The route from Wêreldsend, through Warmquelle and Sesfontein, to the mouth of the Hoanib

150mm rainfall line

Area where rhino are found

Relief in metres

1200

0

## THE DESERT ELEPHANTS

70 true desert elephants live west of the 150mm rainfall line

120 elephants, the transitional population, live east of the line but their dry season movements bring them west of it, into the desert

150 elephants, the eastern population, never enter the desert but move to and from Etosha National Park

*Ugab River*

*Ugabmond*
Rudi and Blythe's home

▲ *Brandberg*

0        km        100

150mm

For Garth Owen-Smith, my friend and guide in the desert
and Dawn and Nancy,
who have never been there
and for Tracy Butler

# 1

# A Far Country

I was still in Johannesburg, that brittle city, in mid-May when the first shock of winter hit. A grey, opaque sky huddled close to the ground and a freezing wind swept from the snowbound peaks of the Drakensberg uninterrupted across the plains of the highveld, down city canyons and into my bones. The cold was accompanied by unseasonal rain, insufficient to break the drought that had bankrupted farmers and threatened serious cuts in hydroelectric power supplies, but enough, when combined with the cold, to depress the spirit. Out on the streets, in the wake of the climatic assault, red noses blossomed like wild flowers in spring.

The previous Friday a car bomb had ripped a hole in the heart of Pretoria, killing eighteen and injuring over two hundred. Three days later Impala jets of the South African Air Force made a retaliatory strike against African National Congress bases near Maputo, the capital of neighbouring Mozambique, thus signalling a vicious new round in the region's tit-for-tat killings. Reports on all fronts predicted a long, bitter winter.

There was nothing to keep me in Johannesburg; it was business affairs that had taken me there and they were now complete. With the arrival of winter I had one more reason to leave the urban malaise and its dreary mercantile mentality as far behind as possible. To that end I had managed, with some difficulty, to make radio contact with an old friend from my Etosha days, Garth Owen-Smith, at Wêreldsend (Worlds End), his Damaraland base camp in north-western Namibia, where he worked as chief conservator for a privately funded organisation, the Namibia Wildlife Trust. There he patrolled the wildest, least developed and most thinly populated tracts of land on earth; a desert expanse larger than the Netherlands and a country with a remarkable story to tell. Garth's invitation to visit had been a standing one and the thought of making the trip never far from my mind. Till now other matters had always intruded but over the radio Garth told of an impending visit to Johannesburg to attend a wildlife symposium, when we might get together and discuss details. We arranged to meet at a Hillbrow restaurant then signed off in a burst of static.

The evening of the meeting I parked some distance from the restaurant and walked the rest of the way along Hillbrow's mean streets, past apartment high-rises, neon-

Left: *Herero mother collecting water, with her infant slung in a goatskin carrier*

bright shopping arcades, past residents and gawkers, some soliciting, others buying, voices forever raised, boisterously, angrily or simply to draw attention. A lesbian twosome, thickset as earthenware, pendulous unsupported breasts rolling under their T-shirts, glared at me with fierce defiance as they clumped by arm-in-arm, daring me to register surprise or disapproval. At a streetcorner bar two men burst from the swingdoor entrance, heavily grappling. One had the other bent over with his arms locked behind his back. They were joined by another man, who looked the situation over and advised, 'Kick him in the face;' then saw me and snarled, 'What the hell are you staring at?'.

'At what's going on,' I replied reasonably.

'Get lost,' and he started towards me. I shrugged and moved away as nonchalantly as I deemed safe. Strange to say, the brawlers were decent enough looking; one wore a T-shirt featuring a coat-of-arms with 'Rhodesia' emblazoned under it – that was probably the answer. With Zimbabwe attaining independence many white ex-Rhodesians had come south and they were full of rage. Anyway, private wars waged in public places are part of Hillbrow's way of life and a fine example of the combustible 'density behaviour' that accompanies overcrowding.

I arrived at the restaurant ahead of Garth and was well into a stein of German lager when he appeared at the reception desk. He looked just as he had on the last occasion I had seen him, with hardly any concession to the fact that he was now in a city. He is tall and bony-lean with a long down-thrust nose that sharply bisects his face. The diffident, unsure smile he offered the head waiter was all but smothered behind a heavy, dark beard. He had neglected to have his hair cut, which, cavalierly shaped in the past to resemble an old doily left out on a rock to dry, hung over his ears, down to his collar at the back. His jacket was shapeless; his baggy trousers bagged at the knees then wanly stopped several inches short of his scuffed desert boots. He peered about with bloodshot eyes too long exposed to the glare of the African sun that have, in consequence, retreated behind shrouded folds of skin. In the smooth-functioning bustle of the restaurant Garth looked ill at ease and hopelessly out of his environment.

We had originally met in 1972 on an Italian liner plying between Sydney and Milan, although we were both returning to Africa and disembarked at Cape Town. Garth had looked striking even then, and amongst the other passengers strikingly out of place – a mountain man cast up in suburbia. I had been intrigued and had sought him out. In our talks he had spoken obsessively of a parcel of land in the far north-west of what was then still known as South West Africa, called the Kaokoveld, a piece of the planet I had only vaguely heard of. He described, in a quiet, even voice that barely concealed a molten intensity, a remote harsh paradise that had remained largely unexplored well into the second half of the twentieth century, protected as it was by an inhospitable coastline and the arid rugged nature of its interior mountains.

He had been hurrying back to that bounteous desert where spiritually he had buried his heart and where, with the pending publication of his comprehensive ecological report on the region, the first definitive study of its kind and fifteen years later still a standard reference work, he was to lay the foundation for his present considerable reputation. Yet it was the manner of his departure from the Kaokoveld that provided the ominous metaphor for the holocaust that was to overcome that fragile land. After two and a half years spent camping out in the trackless wilderness he had come to love, familiarising himself with the country, its wildlife and nomadic pastoralists, he had been precipitately expelled from the territory for attempting to uphold the law, albeit a law that was widely and generally disregarded. His banishment coincided with the beginning of the end for the Kaokoveld's great game populations.

As a young man Garth had trained as a forester in Natal and in 1968 he was appointed to the Kaokoveld as an Agricultural Officer attached to the Department of Bantu Administration. He had been based in the administrative centre of Ohopoho, a Herero word meaning 'the end', implying that this piece of land, and no more, would be given to the whites. At that time the Kaokoveld was the least accessible and the least known region in Africa south of Zaïre, a situation that remains true to this day. Big game was still plentiful then, within the limits imposed by the arid environment. In his survey Garth estimated between 700 and 800 elephant; rhino occurred throughout the central and western districts with a total population of up to 150; 2500 Hartmann's mountain zebra concentrated in the escarpment and semi-desert zones while perhaps as many as 4000 plains zebra roamed the interior plateau. Kudu, gemsbok, springbok, and black-faced impala numbered in the thousands, in turn supporting the many lions, leopards, cheetah, hyena and jackals that preyed on them.

Yet all was not well in paradise. In spite of having 'game reserve' status the area was used by visiting top government officials as a private hunting reserve. Their example was followed by the local officials, who, though legally entitled to a limited 'pot' licence, routinely exceeded it. The territory's senior resident administrator was the Bantu Affairs Commissioner, a feudal power in the land, under whose authority Garth fell. When, in his capacity as Agricultural Officer responsible for nature conservation, Garth had on three occasions followed up cases of excessive hunting, one involving a South African Cabinet Minister, he had been warned not to pursue the matter. 'If you go ahead with this,' the local chief of police had advised him, 'you'll be out of the Kaokoveld tomorrow.' But Garth refused to back away and shortly afterwards, in November 1970, the police chief's prediction was borne out – without any reason being given, Garth found himself transferred to a sawmill in Zululand, as far from the Kaokoveld as it was within the department's power to move him. There was no appeal and, realising he was beating his head against a wall, he resigned his post.

No charge was ever laid in these cases, but a few months later the son of the Commissioner was charged and convicted with illegally transporting a large number of springbok carcasses across the foot-and-mouth veterinary control line into Ovamboland – although he was not prosecuted for the actual killing, that crime being too commonplace to justify mention. The mentality of the time encouraged the killing of game as a natural bounty and a heedless free-for-all rapidly ensued. Let loose in a wildlife treasure house the majority of men appointed to safeguard the Kaokoveld embarked on a hunting frenzy, the profligacy of which astonished the resident tribes who bore witness to it.

But at the time of our original shipboard meeting it had still been early days, and even Garth had not comprehended how desperate the situation in the Kaokoveld had really

Overleaf: *Mountain zebra herd in the Namib Desert*

become. He had been young and strong and full of optimism that it could yet be saved. And determined to return.

During the long, rough crossing he had spoken of his past and his hopes and plans for the future, all of which centred on his vision of a sacrosanct desert Eden. 'No place like it in the world,' he had said, his voice soft with remembrance. 'Utterly unique, and I don't use that word lightly. Great chunks of country that are blanks on a map. Europeans can't get in without a permit so the tribes are unspoilt by contact with western civilization and although most of it is desert or semi-desert, it's full of game. I'd reckon there are more elephants in the Kaokoveld than in the Etosha Game Reserve.'

We had parted ways in Cape Town; from there he had gone on to Windhoek, the Germanic-flavoured rustic capital of South West Africa, joined the State Museum and, in the company of ethnologist Dr J.S. Malan, made two expeditions to the Kaokoveld to study the ethnobotany of the region. This new scientific field involved classifying the native names of plants and how the indigeneous peoples made use of them. The Kaokoveld's pristine spaces presented a rare opportunity to establish the cultural significance plants had as ancient herbal remedies, traditional handicrafts and food, before the old order inevitably weakened and gave way to the new. Until then its remoteness, and the natural conservatism of the tribespeople, had restricted the diffusion of technological man's influence to the fringes of the white settlements at Ohopoho and Orumana. Then almost overnight political tinkering brought into place changes of momentous significance.

In 1962 the South African government, in line with its policy of creating independent black homelands, established a Commission of Enquiry into South West Africa, referred to as the Odendaal Commission after its chairman. It included among its recommendations the deproclamation of the 55,000 square kilometre Kaokoveld game conservation area except for a 32 kilometre-wide strip down the Skeleton Coast, and the ceding of more than half of the Etosha Game Reserve to the proposed Kaokoland, Damara and Ovambo homelands. In 1970, when the recommendations came into effect, they brought about the dismembering of the world's largest conservation area. Proclaimed in 1907 under the German colonial regime by Governor von Lindequist, Game Reserve No. 2, as it had been known, had originally stretched over more than 80,000 square kilometres from east of the Etosha Pan westwards through the wild mountains and lion-coloured plains of the Kaokoveld to the Atlantic Ocean. In spite of representations and carefully researched alternatives put forward by dismayed conservationists, the new demarcations went ahead. In a press release the government attempted to mollify its critics with the assurance that: 'The Minister of Bantu Administration and Development will . . . at a time convenient to both parties, negotiate with the Natives concerned in regard to the establishment of a game park in their homeland. In the meantime conservation of fauna and flora will be carried out according to the existing S.W.A. legislation and, if necessary, special steps will also be taken.' Nothing of the sort ever happened and to this day those promises go blowing in the wind.

Shortly after the legislation necessary to solidify the new boundaries had gone into effect, Garth met June Ade, who soon became his wife. The two made an extensive trip through Namibia, across the international border and on to the southern highlands of Angola. Neither was familiar with this West African state that, at the time of their arrival, was involved in the bloody termination of five hundred years of Portuguese colonial rule. In spite of the human conflict that raged all around they found themselves exhilarated by the untamed grandeur of the place, from the south-western deserts of the Iona National Park to the mountain streams and miombo woodlands of the Humpata Plateau. In the lawless period leading up to and following independence much of Angola's wildlife would be slaughtered, often by soldiers using automatic weapons, but at the time Garth saw little evidence of what was to come and gloried in the country's wildness. It was all he could ask for and June fully reciprocated his enthusiasm.

War conditions make for uncertainties but the one contingency the pair had not allowed for occurred – June fell pregnant with the first of their two sons. On their return to Kaokoland Garth concluded that given the territory's lack of infrastructure it was no place for a newborn baby and reluctantly left to accept a post in Zululand, pioneering southern Africa's first diploma course in nature conservation specifically created for black students. But as far removed and busy as he was, he kept abreast of developments in Kaokoland and the news filtering out of that threatened enclave was increasingly troubling.

When we at last met again in 1980 in Etosha, Garth was silent on the subject of Kaokoland and I, full of the wonders of Etosha, could talk of little else. If I had given it any thought at all I might have imagined the Kaokoveld to have been merely a phase that he had by now passed through. In fact, Garth's silence masked a sense of loss, of anger and pain at the destruction of wildlife, the abuse and neglect that had ravaged Kaokoland during the intervening years. He keenly felt personal failure in that he had not been there fighting to prevent it. What he knew had made him silent, his emotions too inflamed to articulate.

From Etosha I had gone on to explore Zululand's parks and wild places while Garth had left the Department of Nature Conservation to join the Windhoek-based Namibia Wildlife Trust, an association formed in 1982 by a group of conservationists alarmed by the wilful slaughter of game species in Namibia. As a first step, the Trust had worked out a programme of protection for the large mammals of the desert regions, in particular the elephants, rhinos, giraffe and mountain zebra occuring outside proclaimed game reserves in the Kaokoland and Damaraland tribal areas. As Senior Field Officer, Garth was responsible for determining the status and distribution of the endangered species and for spearheading an anti-poaching campaign. It was at that point in our lives that we came together again in, of all places, a Hillbrow restaurant.

'The situation's pretty grim but by no means hopeless,' Garth told me over his Wiener schnitzel. 'It has literally been bloody murder for the game up there till now. What with wall-to-wall poaching and a five year drought, the herds have been decimated – but it's not all bad news. The rains this year haven't been brilliant but enough to get the grass growing again and we've started in on the poachers. Remember Chris Eyre from Otjovasandu in Etosha? Well, he's Nature Conservation's senior man in Damaraland now and he's doing a great job. The enforcement of game laws has taken on real meaning. We've nailed a few poachers and the rest are treading much more warily. And, very important, those we've caught have all been convicted and most have been given pretty stiff sentences which is very encouraging considering that until recently the courts, along with everybody else, regarded poaching as a national pastime rather than a crime. So attitudes *are* changing, not least of all among the general public. The local press has cottoned on to what's been happening and they're screaming their heads off. Now the South African media and conservation bodies have picked up the story so the limelight's really on us. No-one in authority can afford to turn a blind eye to what's going on any more, not like in the good old days. From now on they're going to be held accountable.'

Garth stared at his untouched dinner; 'Don't get me wrong,' he said, looking up and laying down his fork. 'I'm not suggesting it's all easy sailing for the future. Not by any means. We've got an enormous area to cover and we're stretched very thin on the ground. But we've made a start, that's the important thing. Now it's up to us. It's going to mean strict law enforcement, education, the raising of public awareness and a bloody lot of work. Oh, and fund raising; we never seem to have enough money to do even the minimal things needed to be done.'

He made a pass at his food then looked up again. 'You know, some people are saying that it's already too late, that we're fighting a lost cause. They're calling for a rigid ordering of priorities, insisting that all conservation resources be poured into projects with the best chance of success, allowing the rest to go to the wall. They think of themselves as the new pragmatists and maybe they're right, but the northern Namibian deserts aren't necessarily doomed although it's that kind of thinking that'll finish them off. Look, I'm the first to admit that the game's taken a terrible hammering but the point is, there are still viable breeding populations of all species, at least in Damaraland there are, anyway. Given the proper protection their numbers will bounce back and the overflow from these nuclei will move out and restock areas from which they've been extirpated. You only have to look at the white rhino in Umfolozi, and the history of the buffalo and elephant in Kruger and Addo, to realise that under the right circumstances wild animals have an incredible ability to recover from the brink of oblivion. And remember, in Damaraland we're not just talking about any wild animals. These are *desert* elephants and rhinos, for God's sake. The combination of those species and that environment is not found anywhere else in the world. You can't tell me that ecologically and aesthetically they aren't a priority, that they're not worth saving. What a waste, what a loss to science and the world if they're allowed to pass from the scene at this stage, when it's still within our power to do something about it.'

On that note of incredulous outrage Garth finally turned to his food. In the silence that followed I studied my friend, this obsessive, old-world, remarkable man. Like the elephants and rhinos he seeks to save, Garth himself gives the impression of strength, combined with aching vulnerability, and, increasingly, of being outmanoeuvred and out-of-time. Bearing witness, as he has, to what it had once been like and seeing it all so suddenly collapse has left him old beyond his years, yet the experience seems to have provided him with a seemingly endless flow of energy.

I had finished my meal just as Garth started his. He ate hurriedly, without savouring,

Right: *Rhino cow in the harsh Damaraland environment in which they thrive*

merely taking on fuel. He disposed of the congealed hotchpotch before him with the same preoccupation he would have had it been freshly served. His disinterest in food was in direct counterpoint to my appreciation of it. In matters of good cuisine, as in most things, we are complete opposites.

We make an odd couple, a bizarre blending of the hedonist and the ascetic. If it is true that opposites attract, we are surely that phrase's living embodiment. I have followed my enthusiasms wherever they have taken me, grabbing at what came my way with both fists. Garth, on the other hand, has served goals, has soldiered on through disappointments and setbacks, painfully absorbing the body-blows providence has dished out, punishments I have artfully sought to sidestep. We are about the same age, but ages apart. He is prematurely old whereas I, as has often been pointed out to me, have never grown up. I am a modernist with a respect for the past; he is of the past, a stranger to his own era. Our one point of contact was our mutual love of nature and the firmly held conviction that the old tribal values, unsullied by the nebulous ideals of the new Afro-European culture, are owed a place in the sun. It seemed a tenuous link on which to base a protracted expedition into the desert, where the inevitable discomforts, irritations and grievances concomitant with such a trip could only further exacerbate our differences. But there were no doubts in my mind. I wanted to make that journey into the desert as much as I had ever wanted anything in my life and I wanted to make it with Garth Owen-Smith. If I was to travel to a secret place, who better to have as my guide than its guardian, the rough-and-ready fellow sitting opposite me?

'Well,' Garth said, 'there you have it. I shouldn't make so much of the elephants and rhinos, I suppose. Really, what we're talking about here is an entire ecosystem, and if you care about the Himbas and I do, a whole way of life. But the big game are totems, high-visibility symbols if you like, something substantial that everybody can relate to and identify with. And bloody marvellous in their own right. Look around you – people living cheek by jowl, and in a lot of the popular game parks it's not much better, what with traffic congestion and littering.

'When are we going to realise we cannot afford to ignore the importance of wild land? It's a national resource and, given the increasing pressure of urban living, a recreational necessity. If man's war against nature continues, we'll end up in a blighted and decaying wasteland. The signs are all around us, yet we carry on the war in the face of all evidence that in so doing we are rendering our habitat uninhabitable.'

Garth shook his head in disgust, his exasperation temporarily exhausted. The experience of watching mismanagement, stupidity, avarice and political expediency defile the Africa that was, has left him with many embittering insights and deeply imbedded, thwarted passions. Since then, he has single-mindedly committed himself to championing the cause of conservation in the long-standing conflict between separate, colliding worlds. And though the man himself may be addicted to the past, his ideas and proposals are unswervingly progressive. He strongly argues that to be successful goals must be reasonable; that what, from a conservation point of view, is desirable, is not always feasible. When the debate still raged red-hot, he became an early adherent to the hard-nosed school of thought advocating scientifically monitored culling programmes where they became necessary. He supports recreational hunting as a legitimate utilization of a natural resource and has, in his time, done his own share of shooting for the pot. He recognises that the deaths of individual animals are irrelevant in the greater scheme of things; it is the silence and finality that accompanies the death of species and habitats that is so criminal.

'You should come up and have a look for yourself,' Garth said finally. 'See what you make of it. If nothing else, I think I can promise you one or two sights of a lifetime. And,' he added, with a small smile, 'if you don't leave it too late, there might still be a few elephants left to show you.'

The final arrangements for my visit fell into place so quickly that it was with mild surprise that I found myself being driven one sub-zero predawn morning, a few days later, through Johannesburg's eastern industrial townships, past milk delivery vans and fanatical joggers, to the international airport. The man who had kindly offered me the lift in spite of his better instincts shrieking out that he remain in bed was Peter Lind, another old ex-Etosha friend, in Johannesburg for a few days on a business errand that he had, as always, managed to sweeten with a generous side serving of congenial living. Peter, who presently runs a private game ranch in the Eastern Transvaal, looks back on his Namibia days with a great affection and had come within an inch of taking some of the accumulated leave due him, to join me on what would have been for him a nostalgia trip; 'Just to see how the fellows still left up there are surviving.'

While in charge of the Conservation Department's game capture team, Peter had set an all-time record, one that stands to this day, for the total head of game caught and translocated in a single season; and had done so with a below average mortality rate. 'On a good day we were herding, corralling and truck-loading over 150 zebra. Things are a lot tamer down here, I can tell you. Still, here I can get on with the job without all the bullshit I had to put up with there.' For in spite of, or, very probably, because of his successes, Peter fell victim to the petty interpersonal jealousies and intrigues that plague most government departments. Disdaining to engage in the back-stabbing rivalries and corridor politics left him increasingly isolated. It was not enough, he found, to get the work done in the belief that results would speak for themselves. With growing frustration and despondency Peter saw how the internecine sniping was hamstringing his only concern, the capture operations, so, with no relief in sight, he finally threw up his hands and, regretfully and in great disgust, walked out. He resisted appeals to return – 'Nothing will have changed' – and went on to overhaul ecologically his own small private fiefdom, a task that continues to afford him much pleasure and satisfaction. But he still talks animatedly about Namibia's great herds and wide open spaces, the good times and adventures he had there; unable to bear a grudge, the unpleasantries have faded to a dim inconsequential memory.

'Give my regards to Garth and Chris,' he said, helping me to unload my not inconsiderable paraphernalia from the trunk of his car. 'Those two old bastards are probably so "bushed" by now they won't even remember me,' and the thought of his distant friends, blitzed by sun and loneliness, civilization's thin veneer finally forsaking them, caused him to laugh loudly in amusement and empathetic camaraderie.

At the customs check-in the briskly efficient, formidably-coiffured ground hostess looked at the scale bearing my suitcase, sleeping bag, camera cases and tripod, looked again, winced, then thankfully saying nothing, passed them through. I had time for a quick cup of coffee and stood sipping, staring out of the departure lounge window as a diluted sunrise broke over the ground crew hurrying to ready our aircraft. When the boarding call came I stepped from the cheerless overheated terminal back into the sharp bite of the still, frozen air, relieved that soon I would leave both far behind.

My fellow passengers were mainly businessmen with a sprinkling of uniformed soldiers returning to border duty to play their part in South Africa's seemingly interminable, low-intensity bush war against SWAPO (South West African People's Organisation) guerillas fighting for self-rule. Below, neatly ordered suburbs slipped by; multiple blue swimming pools prominent in backyards that, burnt by frost, were as bare-brown as chicken runs. Patches of ground mist trapped in low-lying areas awaited the sun to hurry them on their way.

From the back of the plane a booming American voice cut through an otherwise subdued murmur, and I marvelled how in spite of foreign policy reverses and economic recession the public persona of Americans abroad has clung tenaciously to the buoyant self-confidence of the-sky's-the-limit mentality of twenty years ago. In the row of seats ahead a small boy had turned round to appraise me with the unselfconscious curiosity of children everywhere. I smiled at him but it was more than he could bear and he wriggled out of sight. He must have thought me funny for I heard him giggling to himself until his mother snapped at him to behave. Then breakfast was served. I had been hungry but one sampling of the gelled scrambled eggs put an end to that.

At 35,000 feet we crossed the western Transvaal and the green, looping Vaal River. Off to one side low-level clouds reflecting the sun looked like nothing so much as burgeoning snowfields, a permafrost tundra extending to the horizon. Then the clouds were behind us, replaced by a sea of red, wind-sculpted dunes – the Kalahari thirstland. It was amongst those dunes, in the bed of the fossil Mata River which, millennia ago, had scoured a passage through them, that I once watched a female cheetah with five half-grown cubs streaming at her heels, chase and miss a lone springbok ram; spent daylight hours reflecting upon the sublime nerveless torpor of the almost exclusively night-hunting Kalahari lions – great predators that, hard-put to make ends meet in their uncompromising desert home, have responded by including a significant proportion of porcupine in their diet. And it was in the Kalahari, years ago, that I first came face-to-face with a full-blooded Bushman. He had stood in the shade of an ancient sundered camelthorn, awaiting my approach with seemingly infinite patience and, I thought, a demeanour resonant with bodeful prescience. The wizened old man's tanned apricot-coloured countenance and finely pointed ears I instantly recognised from the legends of my childhood, stories heard in the passage between wakefulness and sleep that are indelibly imprinted on my subconscious. This then was one of the Small People, the Old People, quick with instinct, the progenitor of us all. We neither of us knew the other's language and in truth there was little enough left to say. He regarded me out of bright slitted eyes with the composure of one who has seen the end and I turned to go, leaving him as I first perceived him, muted and unmoving. Once I stopped to look

Right: *Desert elephant cow that died from a poacher's bullets*

back; he stood there still, part of an ageless doomed landscape from which the Great First Spirit had been exiled – turning away for the last time I had felt a terrible sadness.

With the approach to Windhoek came the familiar rugged rolling hills transected by deeply incised watercourses of the Namibian central plateau, and moments later we were touching down.

Little had changed in Windhoek since I had last been there two years before. The curious blend of streamlined contemporary architecture overshadowing buildings of an older German design and the polyglot throngs drifting along Kaiserstrasse, the little capital's immaculate main street, were the same as ever. The more recently introduced body searches at the entrances to department stores had apparently become a regular feature and, given the times, probably a necessary one. I later heard that personal weapons such as handguns are allowed to pass, so presumably it is only incendiary devices that are guarded against.

Garth and I had arranged to meet at the home of a mutual friend, Pieter Mostert, a member of Nature Conservation's information bureau and a bluff, sociable outdoor man in whose company I had hiked and boulder-hopped down the ninety kilometre-long Fish River Canyon. Garth was in town to take delivery of a new Land Rover donated from the proceeds of a fund raising held at the Explorer's Club in New York by the Foundation to Save African Endangered Wildlife. I had heard of the Land Rover's arrival but till then had had no idea who the benefactors were, and on finding out was astonished to have reconfirmed what a small world international wildlife enthusiasts inhabit. One of the trustees for the foundation turned out to be a friend of mine from New Canaan, Connecticut, Michael Devlin, with whom I have swapped many yarns concerning our African experiences without my ever learning of his involvement with the Foundation.

Ignoring the effects of a night overflowing with *gemütlichkeit* Garth and I made an early start the following morning, holding to the tarred highway that runs due north through thicket savanna bounded by steep hills. Before the advent of modern ranching practices this region had comprised broad perennial grasslands but with the installation of artificial waterpoints, year-round grazing had replaced the natural rotational regime of the wild herds and those of the Herero pastoralists. The inevitable overgrazing which ensued created a vacuum that acacia scrub, its growth no longer inhibited by the fierce annual fires of the past, rushed to fill. The end result was the tangle of thorns that now crowds to the road's edge. 'A monument,' Garth remarked laconically, 'to latter-day man's disregard for ecological principles and inability to farm in harmony with nature.'

We drove without stopping through the town of Okahandja, the spiritual home of the Hereros and burial place of Tjamuaha and his successor Maharero, the tribe's first paramount chief; of Maharero's son Uereani, baptised Samuel, who went to war with Germany and lived to see the dissolution of his people; of Friedrich Mahahero and lastly Clemens Kapuuo, assassinated in 1978 by Swapo, when they thought him guilty of seeking common cause with the Windhoek administration. In the blink of an eye we left behind the sleepy outpost that had acted as backdrop to the aspirations and traumas of a proud people.

Beyond Okahandja we began encountering our first large wild mammals; warthogs suspiciously watched our approach then, reassured we had no intention of stopping, dropped back to their knees to continue their ground-level grazing; a pair of unconcerned giraffes stood hard against the gameproof fence of a private nature reserve, employing their 45 centimetre-long tongues to browse the crown of an acacia; a troop of kudu cows and juveniles drifted from sight into the scrub cover that feeds and shelters them.

Frequent road signs – bullet-perforated by idiot gunmen – portraying the silhouette of a leaping kudu warn motorists of the danger of a collision with free-roaming wild animals, but accidents are nevertheless commonplace and each year claim an alarmingly high toll of human lives. On an earlier trip I had been flagged down by a driver whose car's radiator had been stoved in on impact with a warthog breaking cover at the last moment. 'Like hitting a brick wall,' he had said, indicating the collapsed carcass of a big old boar lying nearby.

With 250 kilometres behind us we turned off at the town of Otjiwarongo – Herero for 'beautiful place' – and continued to the mopane-lapped settlement of Outjo that lay prone and motionless in the midday heat. Here the tar road gave way to gravel and heading west on a course that ultimately fetches up on the Atlantic coast we drove on to Khorixas, the administrative capital of Damaraland.

Khorixas takes its name from the Damara word for the sprawling evergreen mustard trees, *Salvadora persica*, bordering the freshwater spring that had allowed permanent settlement. The species is virtually indestructible, a quality the Damaras hoped would apply to their seat of power. Prior to its elevation to capital status the village had been known as Welwitschia, after the weird *Welwitschia mirabilis*, the living fossil plant of the desert which reaches an age of up to 2000 years. Unlike its botanical namesakes however, the village itself is supremely unassuming.

The dusty collection of buildings radiated the sunstruck lethargy typical of desert Africa's frontier posts. Overhung by limp South African flags, the stern facades of the police station and magistrate's court looked incongruous amongst the ramshackle grocery and bottlestores. The sign above a cubicle-sized office exhorted 'Vote D.T.A.!' while the adjoining office countered with 'Stem Nasionaal!' Presumably business was bad, for in neither of the agencies was there anyone to be seen. But the streets were full of life, a gentle ebb and flow of black-skinned, click-tongued Damaras, some in crisp official uniforms but most wearing raggedy town clothes and an occasional older woman in the ankle length, brightly patterned dress they have adopted with minor variations from the Hereros. They all lounged and gossiped with the easy fellowship of those who have little to do and all day to do it. The few cars that passed ruptured the ambience with their unseemly speed whereas the donkey-drawn carts were quaintly in keeping.

'Chris Eyre's new home,' Garth remarked somewhat dubiously. 'Oddly enough, he likes it here. He's out on patrol at the moment though, so let's fuel up and push on, there's still 150 kilometres to go.'

The further west we drove the drier the country became. Trees petered out except along watercourses, with only irregularly spaced drought-resistant euphorbias adding

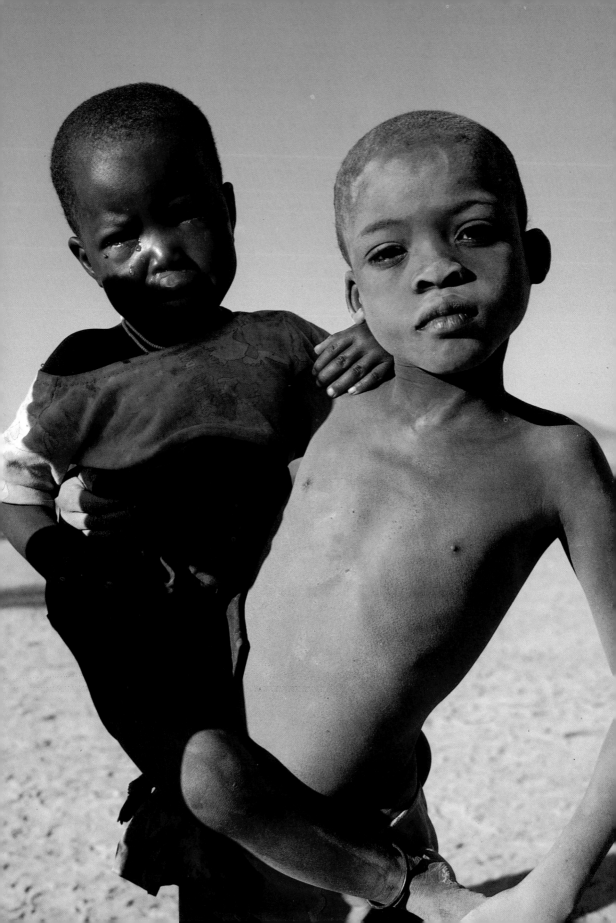

a touch of green to the grass-denuded rocky plains. Towering flat-topped red basalt mesas and pointed spitzkop buttes thrust into a faultless blue sky that went on forever.

These basalt formations and strewn rocks are the solidified lava that covers much of north-western Damaraland and constitutes part of the greatest known volcanic outpouring in the earth's history. Geologically this area dates back over 150 million years to the cataclysmic break-up of Gondwanaland, the mega-continent that had comprised Africa, Antarctica, South America, India and Australia. During that period of fiery transformation, the present basalt had been formed by volcanic lava quickly cooling on coming into contact with the outside air. Yet though science has managed to establish how the land was fashioned, the origins of the current inheritors of the land, the Damaras, remain open to question.

Although they now accept the name Damara, it is one that is foreign to them and until recently they referred to themselves as 'Nu-khoin' or Black People, perhaps to differentiate between their race and the light complexioned 'Awa-khoin', the Red People, as they called the Nama Hottentots. The Namas gave the description 'Dama' to all the dark-skinned tribes of Namibia, calling the cattle-herding Hereros 'Gomasca-dama', the Cattle Dama, while for the Damara they reserved the derogatory epithet 'Chou-dama', the Dung Dama, because of their negligence in burying excrement in the vicinity of their villages. Early European explorers tended to use the Nama terms, but Dung Dama proved too indelicate for their Victorian sensibilities so they modified it to Bergdama, the Mountain Dama, in reference to the tribe's retreat to the mountain fastnesses in the face of constant persecution from their Nama and Herero overlords. However, cultural influences have turned them into quite different people today and they have evolved into one of Namibia's most influential tribes under the innocuous 'Damara' label.

That so little is known of the genesis of the Damaras is not surprising in Namibia, where prehistory must be deduced from folk legends and rock paintings, and racial derivatives from physical characteristics and language roots. In the case of the Damaras the puzzle of their origins is given a further perplexing twist in that of all Namibia's inhabitants they are striking because they have ebony-black skins yet they speak the distinctive 'click' language of the yellow-skinned Khoisan.

Although today the Damaras do not possess a uniform physical type they have retained a homogenous core which suggests that they are a splinter group of proto-Negroid aboriginals that emerged originally in the equatorial forest region of west central Africa, and came south as hunter-gatherers before the continent's Iron Age flourished. Centuries later, with the arrival of Bantu pastoralists pushing down from the Great Lakes district, it seems likely that refugees from these tribes mingled with the Damaras and became fused into one race with them. The outcasts from the east and north introduced the technology of metal-working and thus an exclusive fellowship of Damaras, regarded as magicians by the Namas and Hereros whom they served, became the country's first blacksmiths.

The question that intrigues is, how did it come to pass that the Damara people, without exception, relinquished their own language in favour of such an alien tongue? Undoubtedly the Damaras are the region's earliest black inhabitants, earlier even than

Left: *A dust-covered Herero girl comforts her little sister, distressed by the photographer's presence*

the light-complexioned Namas; they were probably in place before the arrival of the San Bushmen, all of whom were preceded by an extinct Bushmanoid race. The ethnologist Heinrich Vedder postulates that the Damaras came to the Nama language by way of the San, who were related to the Nama and spoke the same language but who lived a hunter-gatherer existence in contrast to the sheep-herding Namas. Forced to flee the depredations of Namas incensed by their stock-raiding proclivities, the San invaded the hunting grounds of the Damaras to the north where, because of their parallel way of life, the two races closely associated. Culturally, however, the San were superior to the Damaras, whom they ultimately dominated and employed as servants.

It may seem strange that the hunting and food-gathering San should have required retainers to work for them but, as Vedder points out, the San of the northern districts understood until early this century how to treat and keep Damaras as vassals. An old Damara once showed him a crumbling elephant pit, saying, 'In this pit I killed an elephant with my assegai but I ate none of its meat for I was then in the service of a San Bushman.'

In the course of time elements of the roaming Nama tribes ventured further and further north, in all likelihood motivated by the need for new grazing for their increasing stocks of long-horned cattle and fat-tailed sheep. Eventually they followed the San across the Orange River and in so doing renewed the age-old struggle between two irreconcilable enemies for available waterpoints and hunting rights, a struggle that now involved the Damaras. Trapped between the better organised Namas in the south and the fierce Hereros in the north, the San and the Damaras were soon reduced to a fugitive, pariah existence.

Piecing together the available threadbare fabric of folklore, explorers' reports and anthropological data relating to the Damara's turbulent history begets a tapestry gapingly incomplete. It would seem probable however that the acculturation of the Damaras and their consequent change-over of languages came about as a result of their relatively benign relationship with the San Bushmen. The process of transition appears to have been well advanced by the time the rapacious Namas made their presence felt. Furthermore, studies done in the earlier part of this century revealed that it was only in the Nama-dominated south of Namibia that the Damaras spoke pure Nama whereas in the northern parts, where at that time they still lived undisturbed in the old way, they spoke the dialect of the San.

The speculation surrounding their evolution is viewed by the average Damara with supreme indifference. Today, as in the past, their concerns are fixed firmly in the present. The matter at hand has always been the fundamental need to survive in troubled times and out of adversity they have created their own recipes for endurance.

# 2

# The Ombonde Giraffe

Night had come to the camp at Wêreldsend before us. Putting aside unpacking till the following morning I joined Garth and his young German assistant Karl Peter Erb, who had walked over to make his introductions, around a pot of strong herbal tea. Without preamble Peter launched into an account of his last patrol, pleased to be able to report the sighting of a herd of sixty springbok in the Uniab catchment. 'I counted at least fifteen fawns, all in good condition'; this was welcome news as the devastating drought of the proceeding five years had radically lowered conception rates amongst herbivores and the few animals born were quick to succumb. The appearance of healthy youngsters meant that the last season's rains, poor as they were, had been sufficient to promote and sustain new life. 'What about rhino?' Garth wanted to know.

'I found the Urunendis cow and calf, both doing well, at the spring and the Swartmodder bull near the junction of the Agab and Uniab Rivers and what I'm sure were the tracks of the young Aub cow at Keikams,' Peter replied. 'Well, if you're right about that last one, she's come a long way from where we first saw her.'

In order to catalogue a profile of all the rhinos sighted, Garth and Peter worked in conjunction with Blythe Loutit, whose husband Rudi was warden of the Skeleton Coast Park, to photograph individual animals and note their sex, estimated age, the shape and size of horns and other distinguishing physical characteristics such as scars or ear nicks. In East Africa field biologists had improved on their identification techniques by comparing frontal head photographs to differentiate between wrinkle contours on each rhino's snout. Not only are snout wrinkles as individualized as human fingerprints but, unlike horns that may break off, they remain constant. This method was simply not feasible in Damaraland however. The open country and extreme timidity of the rhinos made it difficult and, as rhinos were liable to bolt on hearing a vehicle all approaches had to be made on foot, making it potentially dangerous to get close enough for suitable photographs. In fact, given the vast size and rugged nature of the area, the small number of people patrolling it and the rhinos' relatively large home ranges, the chances of even seeing a particular rhino were severely reduced. To help compensate for all the disadvantages the idea had been hit upon of carefully measuring the front and rear tracks of known rhinos and correlating them with spoor encountered during the course of a patrol. It is an inexact system but one that is being constantly refined and updated. Though confusion might creep in where rhinos with the same print dimensions are involved, the movements of animals with distinctive spoors such as a cow and calf or a big bull can be accurately plotted. The sum total of all this painstakingly gathered data would help define a biological portrait of what makes the desert rhino the highly specialised animal it is; what its food and water requirements are, the size of its home range and minimum and optimum densities. The composite picture flowing from this information would be vital when making recommendations for their protection and well-being.

More to the point, if desert rhinos were to survive into the future, keeping tabs on their tracks alerted field staff whenever animals crossed onto a farm or an area with a high human population, thereby dramatically increasing the danger of their being poached. In such instances surveillance in that zone was intensified, a clear signal to potential hunters not to try anything, and it was maintained until the stray returned to a safer locality. Where it had been established that a rhino's home range centred on farmland, contingency plans could be considered for its translocation to a less vulnerable district, a development that would favour the farmer as much as it did the rhino.

When the conversation turned to poaching I asked Peter if he had turned up any signs of it on his recent patrol. 'I didn't come across any new cases,' he replied, 'which doesn't necessarily mean there aren't any. They're going to a lot more trouble to conceal evidence of their kills these days. Still, it does seem to be all quiet on the western front for a change, at least until the next time.'

'If there had been anything,' Garth added dryly, 'it would have been the first item on the agenda and we wouldn't be sitting here now, we'd be out there following it up.'

I didn't doubt for a moment that he meant what he said. To apprehend successfully and prosecute poachers it was essential to get on their trail before they could blend into their communities and dispose of any rhino horn, ivory or meat. If there had been a fresh incident Garth would have insisted on leaving that night in order to be on the scene at first light, and I was glad for both our sakes it wasn't necessary. It had been a long, hot day; Garth was tired and, I realised, so was I.

Queer froggy croakings woke me the next morning – pairings of Rüppells bustards being sonorously sociable before tackling the serious business of the day, the seeking out of sufficient seeds and insects to uphold their standard of living. A Namaqua dove bewailed the state of the universe in a sad, low voice only to be rudely interrupted by a gratingly abusive fiscal shrike, when over all came a boom of laughter, fat and uninhibited – I was about to meet Elias Hambo, Garth's field assistant and right hand man.

Exuding self-assured bonhomie, Elias offered me his hand along with a huge white smile. He spoke no English and we exchanged greetings in the lingua franca of Namibia, Afrikaans, in which he, unlike myself, is fluent. In the months ahead I would come to know and like him well. He is very much his own man; strongwilled, outspoken, with an irrepressible sense of humour and a big laugh. He holds pugnacious, often controversial opinions he delights in expressing. And, as with any well-rounded personality, he has a leavening complement of faults and idiosyncrasies.

Elias' darkly attractive common-law wife, Dina, stood shyly in the background.

Left: *At the end of the drought, once the prey species had died, lions and other predators faced starvation*

When introduced she bobbed her head, murmured something and respectfully averted her large antelope eyes. Elias, talking around a disreputable pipe clenched so firmly in the corner of his mouth that it looked like an extension to his face, sought to dispel the suspended moment by making a gentle joke at his wife's expense. She understood his Afrikaans perfectly well but made no response; her delicate features implied the passivity of a non-participant. In all my dealings with Dina I never knew her to smile or show anger or indeed any emotion other than abiding serenity. She was composed and soft-spoken in all she did and a relentlessly tough negotiator when fixing the price for a month's washing and ironing.

The encampment at Wêreldsend had been built by the Consolidated Diamond Mining Company as an operational base from which their prospectors plumbed the surrounding country. Once their explorations were completed the company had donated the camp intact to the Wildlife Trust. Set down on a basalt-littered plain, it comprised several one-room prefabricated buildings crouched in the shade of a wild ebony grove and surrounded by bare buttes that glowed vermilion at sunset. The windmill blades of a borepump stuck up above the trees, the machinery creaking plaintively as it drew sweet subterranean water to the surface. A collapsible swimming pool standing nearby has on occasion been visited by wandering elephants that come silently at night, ease their monumental thirsts and depart just as unobtrusively.

The small grove is an oasis in that stark landscape and provides sanctuary for a variety of bird species and other lesser creatures. A vegetable patch behind the buildings was keenly watched over by a mob of red eyed bulbuls. Pied crows, those inveterate scroungers, stalked about demanding handouts in loud ruffian voices and a lone kestrel made life hazardous for the buntings and assorted finches that arrived each morning to drink at a water-filled depression. A pair of crowned plovers had set up home on the open ground adjoining the camp, filling the air with electric shrieks of indignation at the approach of a human intruder without ever accepting we meant them no harm.

There was a black cat that lived there; a white-faced female that provided for herself. She was gaunt without being underfed, her condition attributable to a diet of skinks and geckoes. At mealtimes she hovered in the shadows mewing for titbits, but was reluctant to draw close. When scraps were thrown to her she only nibbled fastidiously and without appetite – unlike another cat, a young lion made desperate by hunger, that had invaded Wêreldsend shortly after Garth first arrived there.

In the early stages of the great die-off of herbivores that resulted from the drought, lions and other predators benefitted from the abundance of carcasses. In the desert's fiercely contested struggle for survival, lion cub mortality ranges as high as seventy percent but with food freely available attrition by starvation, that harsh population regulator, hardly applied. Initially carnivores increased in direct proportion to the reduction in the numbers of prey species until inevitably a point was reached where the meat provided by drought victims was used up. In the aftermath there were far too few zebra and antelope left to support the burgeoning lion population and they were forced to concentrate on domestic stock. In one notorious instance an old male even turned to man-eating as a last resort.

At the time of the lion's raid on Wêreldsend the prospector and his wife were still living in the camp. On the night in question they had elected to sleep outdoors to take advantage of the evening breezes. They were fast asleep when the lion sprang across the corner of their bed at the bull terrier lying next to them and seized it by the head. Garth was awakened by the squeals of the dog and the woman's hysterical yells. He understood from her that there were lions in the camp but had no idea how many. Although only one had made the attack there were in fact another six lying up in the sedge nearby but at no time did they play any part in the drama.

Garth cautiously approached the bed which the couple had in the meantime vacated and in the light of his torch the lion calmly returned his stare, the stilled dog hanging from its mouth. Garth first thought to drive the lion away with a vehicle, but in the full glare of the headlights he saw how thin the lion was, a pathetic bag of bones, and realised there was every likelihood it would return the next time it was hungry. That meant one thing, the lion would have to be destroyed. The prospector made the shot, killing it instantly. Miraculously, released from the jaws of death, the bull terrier eventually recovered.

After the rains had come, the herbivores that survived the drought dispersed into the desert leaving the predators stranded. So desperate was their situation that astonishing examples of aberrant behaviour were recorded. A cheetah, which under normal circumstances would have kept well clear of lions, was found feeding on the same goat carcass as a lioness and the two were shot alongside each other.

Near the northern Damaraland village of Sesfontein an emaciated old lion, stunted by malnutrition, its teeth worn blunt with age, attempted in the dark hours of one morning to enter a goat enclosure but was too weak to scale the mopane-log stockade. Wondering at the commotion, the Damara herdsman, himself an old-timer of more than sixty years, came over to investigate and actually saw the lion lying next to the kraal but mistook it for a dog. Giving the matter no further thought he returned to his thatch shelter, never realising that the animal following not far behind was in fact a lion. He suspected nothing until the lion came through the door of the hut and took his wife's arm in its mouth. In that moment of terror and confusion, his head filled with his wife's despairing shrieks, the old man showed remarkable courage and presence of mind. He cast about for his knobkierie but was unable to find it so he picked up a rock and struck the lion in the face with that. The lion immediately let go of his wife and turned on him but it was so enfeebled by starvation that the man managed to pull free. He screamed to his wife to flee with their two year old daughter while he held off the lion, which had reared on its hind legs, by grabbing hold of its mane with both fists. In the dark confines of the hut the old man succeeded in wrestling the lion to one side and made his escape. Bloodied but still functioning rationally he staggered to a nearby army camp where he raised the alarm. The soldiers hurried to the scene and shot the lion as it crouched above a small inert form. Then the old man saw why the lion had not come after him. In her panic his wife had left their child behind; the girl's remains lay beneath the crumpled beast's paws, her head, an arm and a shoulder already devoured.

Tragic as the death of the little girl was, the calamity would have included her parents as well had the lion not been so debilitated. In another incident during the famine a herdsman that came upon a lion feeding off a goat, attacked and killed it with a rock. Most of the lions that did not die of starvation were eventually shot by professional hunters or caught in gin-traps, with jagged teeth that spring together, by Damaraland's farmers, the only course that remained open once their maraudings assumed plague proportions. In all, no less than 76 lions, 33 cheetahs and seven leopards were wiped out in Damaraland alone. There was no choice; hunger had made the lions desperate and bold. They lost their natural fear of humans and with their depredations introduced a reign of terror to the land. It would be unreasonable and unrealistic to expect subsistence stockfarmers to suffer what were, for them, often catastrophic losses, usually without hope of compensation, and not demand the death of the killers.

At the height of the lion problem, Garth visited one family who, having first lost half of their flock to the drought, a few nights before had a pride of 14 lions break into their stock-enclosure and in a frenzy of killing account for 96 sheep and 17 goats, fully half of all the animals the family still possessed.

The impoverished farmer was in a towering rage. 'First God buggers me around,' fumed the normally religious man in an outburst of heresy, 'then the conservation people also bugger me around. I farm in a zoo; my goats are now in the garage where my car should be, elephants rub up against my house at night and the rangers only pretend to shoot the lions. My wife is terrified by the whole business and insists that we leave.'

A few nights later lions again prowled around the homestead, grunting their frustration when unable to reach what remained of the flock. This time the farmer managed to scare them off with shots from a borrowed .303. But it was the last straw; his wife's pleas prevailed and they abandoned their farm and fled the district.

Although Damaraland's large predator populations experienced a devastating crash during the cataclysmic drought years, the ability of carnivores to 'bounce back' under favourable conditions is well documented. Once good rains promote the recovery of the prey species it is anticipated that the surviving nuclei of lion and cheetah will breed up to the inbalance densities existing before the plentitude of drought victims triggered their disproportionate increase.

Africa's wildlife evolved over 70 million years to withstand the cycles of good rain years and drought, predation and exponential increase. Nature saw to it that though individuals died, cycles and species endured. Patterns and processes were perennial and a harmony was created where death was a part of life.

With the appearance two million years ago of primitive hominids a new factor was introduced to the natural equation but one that at the time was absorbed into and made part of the established order. It was not until their descendants developed and proliferated that the eons-old systems were disrupted, at first marginally and later ruinously. Today a more massive death stalks the old continent – the extermination of species and habitats at a rate of acceleration unprecedented in the earth's history.

In the past, man killed only for his life and food. Hunting used to be a low-level affair; there were far fewer bellies to provide for and the relatively unsophisticated techniques limited the rate of attrition. The acquisition and indiscriminate use of firearms changed all that. Human densities increased at the same time as the wild herds

Above: *The ubiquitous donkey cart – chief mode of transport in rural Damaraland*

Below: (left to right) *the author, Elias Hambo, Johan le Roux, Fergie the dog, Garth Owen-Smith and Chris Eyre*

withered away. Arable land was appropriated for agriculture and ranching and later for industrialisation. Expanding mankind and his endless, self-perpetuating needs had to be accommodated. Forests were cleared, the animals shot or driven off, the tribesmen tidied up, put into overalls and taught a nine-to-five routine. The landscape was modified beyond recognition.

What at present remains of the wildlife is bounded by park fences or subsists on land so poor that technological man has not yet dreamed up a use for it. But even here it is not safe. Within the past three decades hunting for the pot, destructive enough in its own right given the number of pots waiting to be filled, has been superseded by mass slaughter for profit. Poaching has become big business. The commercial incentives generated by the illicit rhino horn, ivory and pelt trade tempt not only the nomadic pastoralist, who until recently co-existed with the game, to try his hand, but have spawned organised gangs often using vehicles and automatic weapons.

Garth Owen-Smith's reports to the Wildlife Trust on the situation in Damaraland and Kaokoland dryly record the facts – a phlegmatic chronicle of the decline and fall and eventual virtual elimination of species after species. In conclusion he noted that: 'The populations of all large indigenous mammal species have decreased dramatically in recent years. The reasons for these population crashes can be summarised simply as illegal hunting and drought. In the cases of mountain zebra, gemsbok, kudu and springbok the major cause of their decline was undoubtedly the 1979–81 drought (in effect, the worst ever recorded). Hunting probably also played a significant role for, as the game was forced to move into more inhabited areas, many would have been killed by the stock owners, the majority of whom now own modern rifles.

'Elephant, rhino and giraffe were relatively unaffected by the drought. In fact rhino calves were born when conditions were almost at their driest, and survived. It must be concluded therefore that the declines in their populations – which started well before the dry cycle began – are due almost entirely to illegal hunting. This is confirmed by the fact that 106 out of 127 known elephant carcasses and over 30 known rhino carcasses showed obvious signs of having been poached.

'Since 1970 elephant and rhino have been almost exterminated in Kaokoland. In Damaraland all rhino have been exterminated in the east while only a small population survives in the west. Poaching has also taken a considerable toll of Damaraland's elephants.

'To try and identify all of the individuals responsible for the extermination would serve little purpose at this stage. Many of the main culprits are known, although none was ever seriously brought to justice, and some hold high political office today. Suffice to say that what was started and licensed by a few greedy and self-centred whites, has been carried on by no less mercenary black residents. Today these individuals and gangs are the most serious threat to the small pockets of big game that survive. The desperate situation with regard to illegal hunting dictates that the control of that activity receive the highest priority.'

It was on an anti-poaching reconnaissance that I first accompanied Garth into the field, two days after my arrival at Wêreldsend. We loaded provisions (or 'rations' as

Garth would have it) for a week and with Elias comfortably settled on the bedrolls in the back of the open Land Rover, set off shortly after sunrise.

'This isn't a "game run", there are better areas for that,' Garth advised. 'We're going north where there have been poaching problems in the past. We'll look the area over and at the same time let the locals know we're still active.'

We were using the new Land Rover and it was highly recognisable. The head of a tusker bracketed by lion pugmarks was stencilled on the cab's doors and below – 'SAVE – Foundation to Save African Endangered Wildlife – New York – USA'. There were stickers featuring the World Wildlife Fund's panda symbol proclaiming 'Rettet Natur' and another with the silhouette of a rhino overlaid by a facsimile of its track that warned 'Extinction is Forever'. Besides acknowledging the Trust's sponsors, the distinctive inscriptions would be remembered and so help maintain a high profile; creating an impression of constant vigilance acts as a powerful deterrent to poaching.

We held to the gravel public road, occasionally passing haulage trucks or army vehicles that churned clouds of dust. At first I hurried to close my window but I soon stopped bothering. In this type of country it isn't long before one takes dust for granted and accepts it as an unavoidable fact of life.

We had come into mopane woodland dominated by granite kopjes that stood like stone gardens above the formless world all around them. Squat, liver-coloured *Sterculia* thrust between boulders that, strewn and heaped at all angles, looked like an unfinished explosion. Here white-browed sparrow weavers attended their shabby straw nests lodged in the branches of golden-red paperbark commiphoras. A white-backed vulture and a tawny eagle flapped from the shattered carcass of a jackal lying on the shoulder of the road.

The Land Rover, with only 2000 kilometres on the clock, was giving an inordinate amount of trouble. In negotiating a piece of rough terrain the distributor pulled loose from its mounting and in tightening it the timing was altered whereupon the car started staggering. Earlier the speedometer had packed in. 'Land Rovers aren't made the way they used to be,' Garth grumbled. 'We'll have to get it looked at in Kamanjab.' And with no other choice, we pushed on.

We reached the nondescript collection of buildings that constitutes Kamanjab shortly before noon. In the hot winter sun, under a pale blue sky streaked with translucent grey cirrus, the place exemplified somnolence. A radio broadcast Boer country music – love-lorn lyrics and a whining concertina. The only thing that moved was a mongrelised ridgeback that sidled over to lift its leg against the Land Rover's backwheel.

At a grocery store cafe where we hoped to buy lunch we were informed that bread was sold out, as were tomatoes. No cooked food was available as the gas-fuelled stove was out of gas. We settled for a pack of pressed polony and Cokes. The fresh milk they claimed to have in stock turned out to be long-life; their idea of preserved milk was the powdered kind. As the nearest dairy distribution point was 160 kilometres away they had doubtless adjusted their standards accordingly.

The old boy who ran the store was an Angolan Trek Boer, who, as a child in 1928, had returned south with the remnants of his itinerant tribe to be resettled in northern Namibia by the South African administration. During the course of his shopkeeping years he had established a local reputation for his strongly seasoned meat pies and stews. The seasoning, it was rumoured, helped disguise their origin. It was said that not only did he use donkey and goat meat but that he was not above patrolling the highways to salvage animals killed by passing traffic, including zebras and antelope. But apparently his patrons were more amused than offended by the old backveld entrepreneur and delighted in encouraging visitors to sample his wares before divulging their source.

After a long midday siesta the garage reopened. The mechanic looked the engine over and announced that although he didn't have the necessary part he would be able to effect a temporary repair. 'You should have seen me last time you passed through,' he said to Garth; 'On Monday, wasn't it? I had what you needed then.'

Later Garth said to me, 'I've never spoken to that fellow before today but we each know who the other is and what he's up to. He knew I was here on Monday because as a conservator my comings and goings are carefully monitored and someone must have tipped him off. He'd be especially interested in my whereabouts – he's one of the district's principal poachers and everybody around here knows it. He likes to think of himself as a lion hunter but he'll pot anything he gets in his sights. There's no shame in being a poacher in these parts, quite the contrary. These rural folk always lived off the land and old customs die hard.' In tiny country communities law enforcers and law breakers often keep the same company and just as often there is a blurring of the line dividing the two – in some precincts the police have earned for themselves notorious reputations as poachers.

Beyond Kamanjab our route brought us parallel to Etosha's western boundary fence and we stopped to watch three young bull elephants that had broken out of the park cross the road and with ponderous precision step over the metre-high stock fence on the other side without disturbing a strand. From a stand of *Acacia hebeclada* hung heavy with pods a group of giraffe gazed raptly at us before moving off in their elegant slow rhythm. An unseen yellow-billed hornbill gave vent to its deranged sentiments in a high-pitched staccato chuckle.

We left the main road through a service gate that should have been locked but which someone had forced, 'as someone always does, whenever the padlock is replaced', Garth said angrily. 'Poaching was epidemic in this area. Rhino have been completely exterminated and elephant considerably reduced. And still it's going on. It's going to take heavy duty chains and locks to keep intruders out although it probably won't take long before security police and army patrols shoot those off as well.'

Our track followed the course of the Otjovasandu River in an area known as the Five Farms; land which had been bought from white ranchers at the time of the establishment of tribal homelands and included in Damaraland. The intention is to proclaim it a conservation unit but in the absence of a resident ranger the supervision that exists is nominal, and the only meaningful concession to its proposed status is the provision preventing its reallocation as ranchland to prospective Damara tenants. Nonetheless game trails winding down to the river were stippled with spoor –

Right: *New-born giraffe in mopane copse – umbilical cord still attached*

mountain zebra, giraffe, kudu, gemsbok and elephant – although at that time of the
year surface water had dried up and most of the game had been forced to vacate.

The Otjovasandu's deep-sided dry riverbed threaded white sand through
wintergreen forests of mature mopanes. The prospect put me in mind of replica torrent
courses I have known in Botswana, at Sinamatella in Zimbabwe's Hwange National
Park and the Shingwedzi in Kruger. The sense of *déjà vu* was enhanced by the piles of
elephant droppings littering its banks and the desolate groans of agitated grey louries.
A party of red-billed hoopoes clambered amongst the branches, using their long
curved bills to probe beneath perished bark for caterpillars and beetles, cackling
stridently while they worked. Caught out in the open, a lone bush squirrel took note of
our presence, flicked its tail twice in surprise and alarm then dashed out of sight.

'We could run courses here,' Garth was saying, 'and acquaint children first-hand
with natural lore in its essence. Teach them to appreciate the land again, to reaffirm
their kinships with it; instil in them the ecological principles that maintain the health of
the land.' He spoke with real enthusiasm and went on to calculate how best to
implement a programme. I took his effusiveness as a confirmation that, in spite of the
outrages, the setbacks and heartaches and notwithstanding the enormity of the task he
had set himself, the man remained a dogged practitioner of the art of the possible. Or
perhaps he was simply keeping faith – the thought of giving up too hard to
contemplate.

In the riverbed's soft sand we came upon lion pugmarks, not fresh, but the first we
had seen and the discovery pleased us. 'Probably not more than twenty left in the whole
of Damaraland,' Garth said, 'but lions are resilient and if left alone they'll make a
comeback.' Further on lay the fragmented skeleton of a kudu bull; the skull rested chin
first in the sand, mouth agape in mute appeal, the huge spiral horns tilted skywards. We
wanted to believe it had been taken by lions; but it might just as easily have been
poached or died in the drought – we would never know.

On the other side of the Five Farms we stopped at the Kamdescha veterinary control
gate on the 'red line' that quarantines the north of Namibia, where the threat of foot-
and-mouth still persists, from the south. Foot-and-mouth is a highly contagious viral
disease transmitted by cloven-hoofed animals that in the past has decimated domestic
herds although buffalo and antelope have developed an immunity. In the old-fashioned
north the tribal pastoralists superstitiously resisted even having their cattle counted, to
say nothing of allowing them to be dipped or inoculated. As a consequence no
livestock, dead or alive, or any byproduct of a wild or domestic animal may pass south
of the 'red line' although ingenious strategies have been employed to circumvent the
regulation.

As we were entering the affected area our vehicle was not searched for meat as it
would have been had we been departing. After filling our particulars into a register,
Garth checked back to see what other cars had come this way, then remarked, 'These
gate guards have one of the loneliest jobs in the world – only two or three cars a month
go through here.'

To be sociable and to pass the time of day the guards complained without conviction
about the hopelessness of their situation. They were too isolated, one said, sitting

ducks if Swapo attacked. Garth pointed out that they were armed. Yes, but Swapo would come in the night and show no mercy to a government worker. In the meantime the mopane bees plagued them and a lion had been hanging about. But it was only small talk designed to put off our departure and they cheered up wondrously when their efforts to cadge a few cigarettes proved successful. As we left they were lighting up and sitting back down in the shade to their week long wait for the next car to come along.

Continuing westwards we soon picked up the Ombonde River, of which the Otjovasandu is a tributary. The Ombonde, in the style of many African rivers, changes its name as it progresses. Here it is known by the Herero word for the splendid camel thorns (*Acacia erioloba*) that line its banks, but further west it becomes the Hoanib, an old Nama name of obscure meaning. The broad riverbed demarcates the political boundary between Damaraland and its northern neighbour Kaokoland, although with the drought Herero pastoralists have filtered south in search of new grazing and have let it be known they would fight any effort to send them back.

Though the river takes its name from the camel thorn, those trees were dwarfed by the monarchical winter thorns (*Acacia albida*) that towered green-grey above the bed's steep walls. From below, their leaves had been pruned in a precise line by browsing giraffe and their characteristically curled and twisted reddish-brown pods lay strewn on the ground, a nutritious attraction to elephants and antelope. An African hawkeagle, her heavily spotted breast unmistakable, slipped from a high-rise nest and quickly disappeared. Coveys of red-billed francolins scuttled for cover while flights of rock pigeons streaked overhead. Our passage set off explosions of Rüppell's parrots that ricocheted ahead of us shrieking their protests in a high pitched 'chee-chee-chee'.

'Now's a good time to see game,' Garth said. 'Animals come down to the riverbed in the afternoon looking for shade and acacia pods.' But we drove for mile after mile through the Ombonde's yielding sand without seeing anything larger than a pair of steinbok that stood poised for a frozen moment over a cluster of pods before dashing away.

'Sorry about this,' Garth said at last. 'I can't understand it; usually we would have seen giraffe and elephant by now.' His apology in no way disguised his concern. The uneasiness he felt stemmed less from a desire to gratify his visitor than it did from what the absence of big game might portend. Then, as if to dispel the mood of depression, a small group of giraffe hove into sight. They stared at us from a coppice of young mopane, relieving their nervous tension by delicately arching their tails to defecate. As we drew nearer they cantered off in rocking retreat, all except a newborn calf that stood transfixed by the advent of so awesome an apparition into its life. A vestige of umbilical cord still curled on its abdomen and its unformed horns were whimsically fluffy. Focusing on the trusting calf through my camera's viewfinder I thought how easy it would be for a poacher to knock it down.

A little way beyond the giraffe we left the car in the shaded riverbed and climbed a high hill to spy out the land. Dolomite hills ranged all around. On the plains below bright bleached grass was pocked by dark green mopane shrubs, widely spaced. I could see a single browsing giraffe and from near at hand a quarrel flared among a small party of white-tailed shrikes. Garth was trying to recognise a hill where during an aerial

census he had seen a rocky declivity that held winter water, but the land looked quite different from the ground. Walking in search of the pool we came across the desiccated shrunken remains of an adult elephant cow. So deflated was the carcass it looked more like that of a juvenile's but the fact that its sixth (and last) set of molars had already erupted determined it to have been mature. The maternal rounded pelvic girdle indicated her sex. She had died about eighteen months before, during the drought, but was less likely to have perished from natural causes than to have been poached. Her tusks had been drawn and she lay alongside a dried up rainwater pan – an ideal ambush site.

I followed Garth's long loose-limbed stride down a well furrowed game-trail, enjoying the opportunity to exercise cramped muscles. Once Garth stopped to point and say, 'On one of my first patrols amongst those hills I found the gutted shell of a springbok that a leopard had hauled into the fork of a tree. Later I found leopard tracks in the riverbed but I haven't turned up any signs recently – I wonder if it's still alive.'

Cutting across a dolomite scarp our attention was caught by a pair of lappet-faced vultures gracefully spiralling – then another two – then a bird rising. Obviously there was a kill nearby. As we came up we counted through binoculars twelve vultures busy feeding, clustered at the abdominal cavity and on the ribcage of a sprawled giraffe. At our approach they taxied, then flopped into the air, carried aloft by strong heavy wingbeats.

A quick examination was all it took to confirm that the agents of the giraffe bull's death had been humans. The pattern of prints left by the vultures, jackals and hyenas that had been attracted to the two-day-old kill had not entirely obliterated those of man. The thick skin on the giraffe's neck had been neatly pared by the blade of a knife and an egg-sized hole in the ribs could only have been made by a bullet.

It was already late afternoon with too little light left to think of doing anything more that day other than make a report. As we hurried back to Elias and the Land Rover I saw the first of the returning vultures drop from the sky.

While Elias and I set up a rudimentary camp Garth persevered with the field radio, eventually making indistinct contact with Chris Eyre in Khorixas. Chris was at that time the official responsible for all conservation-related affairs in the region. Although Garth had worked as a conservator he was now a private citizen without the authority or the powers of arrest that Chris had. Fortunately Chris was a very good man to deal with. Apprised of the facts, he crisply responded through a storm of static, 'I'm on my way – see you later this evening. Over and out.' During a meal of grilled lamb chops and boiled potatoes I mentioned to Elias that only a little meat and hide had been taken by the poachers and wondered if they might have been disturbed. 'Perhaps, *muhona* (sir),' he replied. 'In this area the hunters are sure to have been Hereros and they eat all the meat on a giraffe. They also cut the legs off at the knees to get at the bone marrows. In the old days they used the hide to make sandals but now only cut strips for sjamboks (whips).'

Warming to the subject, Elias went on, 'Beef is our favourite meat but zebra and giraffe were also considered delicacies. We hunted them with dogs and our bows and arrows. There is some meat we will not eat – such as that of the ostrich – it stinks too

Left: *Examining poached bull giraffe that was pursued on horseback, then stoned and finally shot to death*

badly. But now I have heard that even ostrich is being eaten – it's because of the drought. Once there was enough; now Hereros eat whatever comes to hand. Some even eat donkeys, which they never did in the past. When the donkeys are finished maybe they will start to eat dogs as the Ovambos do. We might even become like the Damaras and Bushmen who gobble down snakes. That wife of mine eats that sort of thing,' he concluded in disdainful reference to Dina, a full-blooded Damara.

We rolled out our sleeping bags on a groundsheet and slept with nothing between us and the stars. A young moon, recurved and shining low in the west, was held like a slender shaving by the silhouetted branches of an acacia. Dramatically the silence was broken by the roar of a lion that sounded about two kilometres away. Without comment Elias got up to add wood to the fire and before resettling he significantly cocked the old .303 he always took to bed with him. A bat detached itself from the shadows to flit to and fro in pursuit of insects attracted by the flames.

At about two in the morning a warm easterly blew up, the result of high pressure in the interior. Shortly afterwards I heard the engine of an approaching vehicle and then headlights rounded a bend in the river. Chris had arrived with Lucas Mpomporo, his long-suffering assistant. There were murmured greetings and I started to rise but Chris said, 'Don't get up – see you in the morning,' and we left it at that.

Our day began before first light with coffee and biscuits around the stoked fire. Talk was subdued, only Chris's fox terrier Fergie was unaffected by the sombre hour and the business at hand. A pearl-spotted owl cried in the dark. To lighten the mood Chris said: 'Well, Elias, these giraffe poachers might be friends of yours; I hear you're an old hunter.' Chris was teasing him but Elias chose to take it seriously. 'Yes, I am a hunter. My father brought me up on zebra meat but I still haven't shot a rhino or an elephant,' he retorted with a barbed hint of anticipation. At that Garth smiled to himself. He was well aware of Elias's background and had once told me that old poachers made the best game guards – they knew all the tricks and the people involved. But he had acknowledged that it would be wrong to believe they would become true converts to conservation ethics; quite simply it was a luxury they couldn't afford and had no relevance where their day-to-day struggle to make ends meet was concerned. As long as they received a wage ex-poachers were invaluable assets to an anti-poaching unit but if the system should ever collapse, and they found themselves jobless, they would probably revert to their old profession. They might have no choice, coming as they did from a stratum of society where the threat of starvation was a constant reality.

As the navy sky turned to grey the riverbed echoed with morning sounds – the hysterical racketing of red-billed francolins shot through by a grey hornbill's plaintive whistles. We finished our coffee and left our camp.

A lion had come to the giraffe carcass during the night, perhaps the same one we had heard broadcasting its challenge. Jackals had eaten the heart, lungs and liver – and very likely the slug that killed the giraffe. If the slug had been recovered it would have been used as court evidence. Instead a hard circular piece of plastic was found that Garth presumed (correctly, as it transpired) to have been the bottom of a quiver. There was a shoe print with a distinctive home-made heel, without any tread, that Chris asked me to photograph. There were also horse and donkey tracks and measurements were taken of three different specimens. 'The donkey tracks you can forget,' Chris declared. 'There'll be any number of donkeys at the village, but they lost most of their horses during the drought, so doing a comparison of the horses' tracks might produce results.'

The tracks in the sand suggested what had happened. The giraffe had been chased and brought to a standstill by a horseman, had then been shot and its meat carried away on the backs of donkeys. The trail of the departing donkeys was easy to follow; where they crossed similar looking zebra tracks they could be distinguished by the 'frog', a mark shaped like an arrowhead enclosed within the shoe, that zebra tracks lack.

It was decided to make the follow-up on foot so as not to alert anyone ahead and we set off in single file. Garth carried his shotgun and Lucas and Elias their old .303s; not that anyone expected trouble but it made sense to play safe, and anyway guns added authority.

About twelve kilometres on we arrived at a small village and when Chris asked Lucas the name of the place he answered 'Otokotorui', the word flowing from his lips like a ripple. It inelegantly translated into English as 'The place of subterranean water', and had recently been settled by several Herero families attracted by the permanent water supply a government-sunk wind-pump provided.

Our sudden appearance in the village set the dogs barking. Ignoring them we headed straight for a man shaving himself with the aid of a hand-held mirror. After a brief introduction, Chris announced bluntly, 'We're looking for the people who killed that giraffe and their tracks stop right here.' The man, who introduced himself as Goliat Tjithempisa, was clearly shaken by Chris' peremptory tone but sought to maintain an outward appearance of nonchalance by coolly continuing to shave. Speaking in Herero which Elias translated, Goliat denied having the faintest idea what Chris was talking about. Another man inquisitively sidled closer. He wore a pair of scuffed high-heeled shoes that had been fashionable a few years before and still remain a big hit amongst Africans. The heels had been renewed by a set of his own making. Chris stared at his footprints very hard and long, and then at the man. 'I smell giraffe meat,' Chris said with quiet menace. The man visibly flinched and looked away. Without another word, Chris turned on his heel and ducked into the low entrance of one of the thatched huts. Goliat started shouting and Elias turned to me and said, 'Goliat says *muhona* Chris mustn't go into his house without first asking his permission.' Before I could reply Chris reappeared with a sack of dried meat in his hand, walked up to Goliat and, waving the sack under his nose, loudly demanded, 'What's this? Now you'd better start talking, I'm losing my patience.'

At first Goliat tried insisting it was meat from a steer that had died but when I explained to him through Elias that laboratory tests could be done proving it to be giraffe meat and as Chris kept turning up more caches of biltong, his denials faltered. He next adopted an air of righteous indignation. Why was it, he asked me, that while I spoke nicely, Chris behaved so rudely? I said that Chris was with the conservation department and was very angry; it was his giraffe that had been killed, not mine. To be honest, I think I also harboured a ludicrous television-inspired notion to play 'good cop' to Chris's 'bad cop'. The ploy turned out to be unnecessary – the game was up and Goliat knew it.

Chris came over and said, 'By the amount of meat I'd say there are two giraffe involved and what looks like a gemsbok; Lucas agrees with me but we'll never get enough evidence to prosecute them successfully for all three. I'd rather go for a conviction on the giraffe we found. Giraffe are specially protected game, so the penalties are higher.' Suddenly he winked broadly and, as if to explain a side of him I had never seen before, said, 'I always come on strong when I start an inquiry and usually it works. The guilty parties get too flustered to dream up alibis.' Then he chuckled self-deprecatingly; 'Right now these people need me like a hole in the head.'

After a quiet talk with Lucas and Elias the men of the village admitted they had all helped transport the meat, in itself a crime, but that the actual hunters were away at the moment. Presumably they were out hunting again as we were assured they would be back before long. So with nothing better to do Garth and I brewed up a pot of tea while Chris took statements.

Two hours later the hunters returned, riding grey donkeys, one of them carrying a slung .303. In the light of developments during their absence they were fortunate in having been unsuccessful on that particular foray. Informed of what we knew the two wasted no time with prevarications. One of them introduced himself as Adam Tjikwara and said that as he had planned it, he assumed full responsibility for the killing. With the confession the tension went out of the situation. Adam asked Chris for a stop of tobacco and everyone settled down to hear their story and have another cup of tea.

'I borrowed a horse from a neighbouring village for the purpose of giraffe hunting,' Adam said, 'then I sent this younger man out to catch one.' Here the other man took up the tale. 'I chased the giraffe till it got too tired to run any more. I didn't have a rifle so I tried to kill it by throwing rocks at it. I hit it here and here', he said, patting himself on the chest and biceps; 'oh, and a rock knocked out its right eye. Still it wouldn't go down. I had to come back here and get a rifle to finish it off.'

It was a simple enough account and the events it described have been enacted with minor variations countless times over the past two decades. Pursuing a giraffe to the point of exhaustion and then stoning it to death is a traditional way of hunting the mild-mannered creature in these parts. And the rifles that the pastoralists have come by are the result of a misguided scheme on the part of the South African army to arm local tribesmen in the unfounded hope that they would use them to repel Swapo guerrillas.

Chris decided to charge the two hunters and let off those who had been in possession of illegal meat with a stern warning. It was a good compromise – to arrest everyone involved would have left the village without any men, a calamitous contingency. As a progressive naturalist, Chris recognised that if the game is to be conserved, it is no longer realistic to disregard the human factor.

Listening to the details of his impending fate, Adam stared at me with old eyes, smiling the saddest smile I have ever seen. Then his gaze dropped from my face to a point on the ground just in front of his feet where he stared fixedly, wistfully smiling all the while.

It was agreed that Chris would take the accused to Korixas for formal charging while

Above: *Tracking the spoor of donkeys used by poachers to transport giraffe meat to their village*

Below: *Questioning heats up, with Goliat giving as good as he gets*

Garth and I visited their headmen Keefas Muzuma and Joshua Kangombe to brief them on what had happened. The case had particular relevance to both chiefs as the young hunter was Joshua's nephew and, by Herero custom, his heir – and he had also been in charge of a herd of Keefas's cattle at the time of the shooting. 'It is crucial if we are to get the support of the chiefs and through them their people, to inform and involve them fully in a case like this,' Garth said as we ploughed down the Ombonde. 'Too often in the past the chiefs' authority was ignored which they naturally resented and so withheld their co-operation. It led to a "them" and "us" situation and a great deal of ill will. Ultimately the key to controlling poaching will lie not so much in arresting the people responsible as in educating them. Prove to them that they too have a vested interest in conservation and can directly benefit from it and you will have solved your poaching problem. The hunting that the white man now calls "poaching" has been around for a long time and it would be ridiculously short-sighted to regard the death of the Ombonde giraffe as morally reprehensible. Legalities aside, there are no rights or wrongs in that case – quite simply it boils down to competition for the same resource. From the comfort of our well-padded perspective we enthuse over the aesthetic value of wild animals whereas Adam, living a lot closer to the cutting edge of deprivation, thinks they should be turned into Herero hamburgers. Different points of view arrived at through different economic circumstances.'

Ahead of us five giraffe broke from the riverbed then pulled up to peer back at the Land Rover. Their relative tameness suggested that what poaching had taken place in the area had been done by the Herero newcomers. Although we had seen very little game it was apparent from the way animals reacted to us that they had not been harassed in the past.

'During my patrols I make a point of keeping in touch with local residents and establishing friendly relations,' Garth continued. 'That way I get to know them and, equally important, they get to know me. In any extension programme among a rural and therefore conservative people, the slow and time-consuming task of gaining their acceptance is vital. If we were to rush in as strangers and start telling them what they should be doing, we wouldn't get anywhere. Worse – if suspicion was once aroused it would take a lot longer to get them to accept us and our ideas.'

Keefas Muzuma held court in the open, seated on a folding chair and attended by a council that hung on his every word. He had a charming gap-toothed smile and a gift for playing to the crowd. An unravelling straw hat perched incongruously atop his massive head, his frame looked disproportionate, shrunken as it was by a recent illness. His weary suppurating eyes slitted against the fierce glare, his deep measured voice and resolute manner lent him an air of ponderous flawed dignity. A translator recounted Garth's news and at the end Keefas considered the implications while everyone waited in silence for his reaction. The old man them said he was sorry to hear what had happened but that he fully supported Chris's actions. He had warned his people against hunting and if they persisted they must bear the consequences. He knew both the men involved very well and it surprised him that such normally reliable fellows should flout the law in the way they had. He thanked Garth for notifying him so speedily and after a formal exchange of pleasantries we went on our way.

Joshua Kangombe was equally understanding even though it was a favourite nephew that was at that moment being arraigned. He made a small speech to an assembly of elders and concluded by saying: 'The law against killing game comes not from the white man but from your headman. It is our wish to protect the game for the good of our people. If we kill it all now there will be nothing left for the future.'

His positive attitude was enormously gratifying and amongst the others there seemed a genuine acceptance of the need for conservation. One old man remarked, 'Everyone knows there is a law against hunting without a permit – they do it when they are hungry. When the stomach growls laws are disregarded. In the past the law was not so strict, perhaps because there was so much game. The young people who are without employment are the main poachers. If the government could provide employment it would help the situation.'

Unemployment, together with the loss of most of their livestock during the drought, added to the failure of the village's entire maize crop that year, were the underlying causes of much of the poaching taking place. It is no use telling local populations not to hunt and expect them to comply without providing an alternative.

Acting on that presumption Garth devised a plan that would create limited jobs and at the same time directly involve the local population in the conservation of their own areas – a major objective as it was the best way to ensure the long-term conservation of wildlife in that region. It was decided that the chief, using his own discretion, would recommend suitable men to work for the Trust as auxiliary game guards. They would be stationed in areas where Garth knew poaching to be particularly bad and would be responsible for making game observations as well as for reporting any poaching incidents that occurred. As they had an intimate knowledge of the area and the people living there, little could happen without their knowing.

Once it was passed by the Trust's management committee the plan was put into operation and has since proved to be one of those low key, low budget success stories. It was pure coincidence that I was in Khorixas the day the giraffe poachers appeared in front of the magistrate. I had come to collect the monthly supplies and, stopping off for a cup of tea at Chris Eyre's office, I learnt from him that the hearing was set for later that morning. Chris looked unfamiliarly scrubbed and brushed for his role as prosecuting officer, acutely aware of the solemnity of the impending proceedings. Like countless other small dramas being played out in the world that day this one was central to the lives of its participants.

The courthouse stood next to a soaring Dutch Reform church. Inside were three rows of wooden benches and I took my place at the back amidst a bevy of Herero women. The ladies wore the brilliant turbans and long rainbow-coloured dresses that are a legacy of the grimly modest German missionaries sent out in the last century to convert the naked heathens. The magistrate and the state prosecutor both wore black gowns. Adam appeared at the witness stand in an old grey greatcoat which he evidently considered suitably formal for a day in court. His co-accused had made the most of his visit to the administrative capital and turned up at the trial weavingly drunk. Perhaps his condition was not regarded as being unusual or out of order, for as long as he remained subdued the magistrate paid him no heed.

Both men pleaded guilty to the charge, then Adam, the only coherent one of the two, said in mitigation that he had six children to support, two of whom were at school. 'We killed the giraffe to feed our children,' he said through an interpreter. 'If that's so,' the magistrate asked, 'why did you leave so much meat behind?' 'We were afraid of the police, so we did not return,' Adam said, although he had originally told us the giraffe was too old and its meat very tough. In fact he had been most surprised we had ever found the carcass. We suspected that poaching had been sufficiently successful to permit the people of Otokotorui to become choosy.

Adam asked that the confiscated rifle used to kill the giraffe be returned to him so that he could protect his family from Swapo. That threat had no basis in reality and his request was sensibly denied. They were then each sentenced to a fine of twelve hundred rand or twelve months in gaol. When Adam asked for time to raise the money, the magistrate granted him six weeks. That ended the session and we all filed from the courtroom.

Outside we found Adam pensively adjusting his old bush hat. He seemed to accept that Chris and Garth had simply been doing their job and bore them no grudge. Shaking his head at his bad luck and smiling his sad smile he said, '*Muhona*, that was a very expensive giraffe.'

Left: *Adam* (right) *and accomplice return from their latest hunting trip*

CHAPTER

# 3

# Desert Elephants

One June mid-morning, looking westward from Keikams Spring, I saw in the distance seven elephants approaching. I watched them through binoculars as they came in single file at a fast stiff-legged walk, straining towards the water. Viewed with the naked eye the shuffling column of great beasts was diminished and overwhelmed by the immensity of the austere landscape. They advanced across a rocky red plain that extended its perfect level to jagged blue mountains on a haze-diffused horizon. Between the herd and their destination the land was empty of vegetation except for an occasional white-barked shepherd's tree. The vast westward prospect enveloped the elephants – they looked like tiny molecules adrift in the hugeness and space of a primordial world.

The sturdy cow leading the group maintained her pace until they reached the cool dense stand of tamarisk that bordered the spring; then they abruptly slowed down. Their passage had in no way disturbed the pervading stillness. In total silence, they one by one filtered out of sight beneath pale green branches. I waited for them to emerge into a clearing on the other side of the grove where a favourite, low-salinity seep was situated; but they remained hidden. It was almost as if having come so far for a drink they were deliberately delaying the exquisite reward. In fact they were analyzing the omens, divining the wind for portents of danger, for the presence of man – the only predator elephants have ever had to fear. The big Damaraland cow's innate caution had almost certainly been reinforced by bitter experience and a spring was too convenient an ambush site to permit a reckless approach.

A steady wind held in my favour and I was able to walk unnoticed along the lip of the steep flood-gouged bank until I came to a point where their grey wrinkled backs were visible just below me. The herd was in all probability a family unit with all its members being immediate relatives. It was led by an exceptionally big matriarch – she looked as robust as an adult bull – and included two mature cows, a young bull and two calves of about four and five years old. They huddled together in companionable close contact, mute and unmoving, as if sunk in deep contemplation. Then a trunk was lofted into the air and like a questing periscope was held upraised for a long moment, the bewhiskered pointed tip pivoting from left to right. As I was downwind my scent went undetected and the trunk flopped down without registering any potential threat. Satisfied that all was well but still maintaining good order the elephants trooped from the sheltering tamarisks to the pool with the least brackish alkaline content and, trunks dipping then coiling, squirted litre after litre down cavernous throats.

At this time of the year the Keikams Spring is a source of life for elephants as well as many other creatures. Its waters rise in the sandy bed of the Achab River where a transverse rock barrier had forced the subterranean flow to the surface. Perennial springs such as Keikams, although not that uncommon, are nonetheless remarkable here in northern Damaraland's arid western regions where the average annual rainfall is less than 150 millimetres per year. Not only is the rainfall ephemeral in this desert ecosystem but the pattern of precipitation is extremely irregular and frequently patchily dispersed. As a consequence primary production is impoverished, which in turn means that because of the flimsy mantle of plant cover, rain run-off is swift, resulting in flash floods. Moreover, the high intensity of solar radiation leads to rapid evaporation. Small wonder therefore that water is the most important single limiting factor for most biological processes in the desert elephant's implacable kingdom.

What the world's largest terrestial mammal is doing in a desert in the first place is an intriguing question. The mere fact of its existence confounds and excites the imagination. One wonders how an animal that needs to eat more than a hundred kilograms of vegetation each day survives in a habitat so atypical, so seemingly lacking in sustenance. There is an enigma about these desert elephants, and a mysticism as inscrutable as the desert itself.

To see a lone elephant negotiating a sea of sand dunes or a herd crossing an endless gravel plain is to be rewarded with one of the great sights of a lifetime. Yet so extraordinary is their presence there that it has led some people to conclude that the phenomenon is less natural than induced. Amongst other things, it has been conjectured by at least one prominent research administrator that the elephants do not really 'belong' in the desert at all, that they have sought sanctuary there in the face of human persecution. He goes further, maintaining that these fugitives have been isolated in their pitiless refuge by a barrier of human activity that prevents them from returning to more benign pastures.

With so little information to hand regarding their ecology, it is perhaps not surprising that a controversy has billowed up around the desert elephants. Some paticipants in the debate argue that the elephants are unique and a conservation priority, while others dismiss them as being nothing out of the ordinary and of no particular interest. Newspapers have picked up the story and reported often unsubstantiated statements, such as that they migrate from Etosha, that their reduction in numbers came as a result of the drought, that they wreak havoc on the fragile desert environment or that they are a distinct subspecies. Predictably it did not take long for the topic to turn contentious. In the rarefied and somewhat arcane world inhabited by wildlife specialists, interpersonal rivalries often run deep. The plight of the desert elephants created the opportunity for brand new philosophies to be tried out against familiar old doctrines. Pragmatists squared off against so-called idealists – prejudices were well to the fore and accusations were hurled like missiles. While all this was taking

place the elephants themselves were being poached at a rate that threatened to make any further discussion purely academic.

Instead of making pronouncements it might be more useful to start asking questions. That not only elephants, but rhinos and giraffes as well, live in what for them represents totally marginal habitat in western Kaokoland and Damaraland is an established fact. The question is, why are they there? Furthermore, how do they survive, do they remain in the desert permanently or are there seasonal migrations; what impact do they have on the environment and do they belong to a special race? To put things into ecological perspective and to understand the biology of the animals involved means observing their way of life in their natural habitat. Recent field studies have helped provide a fascinating glimpse into the activities and adaptations that permit elephants to occupy the northern Namib successfully.

Between 1968 and 1970 Garth Owen-Smith carried out pioneering work on the numbers and distribution of Kaokoland's larger wild mammals. He estimated a total of between 700 and 800 elephants, with 200 to 300 occurring in the western desert regions. He estimated there to be about 150 rhinos, of which approximately half were to be found in the west. Regrettably no reliable survey was done south of the Hoanib River, but at the time northern Damaraland was still part of the greater Etosha Game Park and the area would have protected at least equal densities of big game. By early 1982, however, wildlife populations in Kaokoland and Damaraland had reached critically low levels. An aerial census conducted in the two territories by the Namibia Wildlife Trust indicated that only about 340 elephants remained in total, of which seventy were resident in the west. Rhino had disappeared altogether in the east and the western desert population had decreased to approximately fifty animals. Of these probably no more than five still existed throughout the whole of Kaokoland. In just twelve bloody years poachers had destroyed 97 percent of those immense, strange creatures whose ancestors had browsed that ancient land for sixty million years.

The term 'desert elephant' refers to about seventy surviving animals whose home range lies west of the 150mm isohyet (rainfall line) that extends from the Otjihipa Mountains in the north to near Twyfelfontein in the south. East of the line there are about another 120 elephants that make up what is known as the 'transitional' population, whose dry season movements bring them west into the desert. The balance of approximately 150 elephants constitute the 'eastern' population, members of which move to and from the Etosha National Park. Contrary to the opinion of some commentators, intensive studies have shown that the desert elephants occupy definite home ranges within the desert and do so throughout the year. They do not, as has been suggested, only occupy the desert on a temporary seasonal basis, nor do they feel compelled to extend their range eastwards to the Etosha National Park. Not that there is anything to prevent them moving east should they wish to do so. There is, to this day, a corridor free of human activity that extends right through to Etosha and which is extensively used by elephants from the eastern population. It is apparent that the movement of the desert elephants follows a pattern similar to those of elephants in other parts of Africa, where field research points to a temporary extension of home

Left: *Eighteen-month old elephant foetus – the cow was shot by poachers*

ranges during the rainy season and a reduction during the dry season. Nowhere on the continent does evidence exist that elephants undertake long migrations.

The person best acquainted with Namibia's desert elephants is P.J. Viljoen, nicknamed Slang, who set out to study systematically their social organisation, behaviour and ecology. Working under gruellingly exacting conditions he made continuous observations over a period of five years during which he travelled 150,000 kilometres by vehicle, spent 350 hours conducting aerial surveys and stepped out uncounted kilometres on foot. As his study progressed he was able to plot the desert elephants' movements; how they related and interacted with each other and their environment; and their population dynamics based on reproductive rates, mortality and other factors – an aspect that was dominated by the scourge of poaching. What emerged from his systematic scientific observations in many ways contradicted popular theories and beliefs, but they present a much more realistic portrayal of the mysterious desert elephant.

Viljoen has always been interested in nature and his nickname 'Slang' harks back to a boyhood passion for collecting snakes. He is at ease in wild places – on familiar ground, and able to interpret what he sees. As is appropriate for someone who spends much of his time alone in a desert, he tends to be a man of few words. He is inclined to go about barefoot, even when walking the roughest terrain – a peculiarity that has become a trademark. Most important, he has established a reputation amongst his fellow conservationists for his painstakingly thorough research and sensible recommendations. But he is essentially a very private person who rarely draws attention to himself so that although his is the only comprehensive study of its kind, Viljoen's voice is often drowned out by the clamour of those who refute his findings in order to devalue the northern Namib as a conservation priority.

There is only one way to get the amount of data necessary to describe the ecology of a specific elephant population, and that is to be able to recognize individual animals. To achieve this, Viljoen compiled a photographic record of each and every elephant he encountered in the desert. He found that individuals could be readily identified by such physical characteristics as holes and tears in their ears, tusk formation and degree of wear, and by the pattern of the tail hairs. The combination of these distinguishing features was more than enough to guarantee accurate identification, as no two elephants were exactly alike. He then set about tracking individuals as they foraged across their extensive home range, recording his observations through all seasons including periods of severe drought as well as good rains. In this way he was able to conclude without a doubt that his study group was permanently resident in the desert. Movement patterns were largely influenced by climatic factors that in turn determined the quality and quantity of available food and water. During the dry season the elephants mostly concentrated in the river courses feeding on leaves, bark, twigs and acacia pods, but with the onset of the wet season they dispersed into the adjacent plains in order to harvest the fresh green grass that was sprouting.

Elephants were first reported as having been seen in the desert in 1895 by Oberstleutnant Dr Georg Hartmann during that stalwart gentleman's epic exploration of the lower Kunene and the Skeleton Coast. At that time there were very few people living in eastern Kaokoland, which would discount the notion that human harassment had driven the elephants there. It would appear that they were in the desert ninety years ago simply because they chose to be there and in every likelihood they had made it their home for much longer than that.

The question as to why elephants should resort to a desert habitat in the first place might best be answered with the rejoinder – if they can make a living there, why shouldn't they? Elephants are amongst the most adaptable creatures on earth, able to live in environments varying from lush rain forests to savannas to – as has now been unequivocally demonstrated – deserts. Elephants, in common with all forms of life, fit into such ecological niches as are available. The wide range of plants and feeding levels which are physically available to elephants as food, their catholic tastes and their ability to cover seventy kilometres a day at a comfortable walk, allow them to colonise the desert at low densities because they have no local competitor better equipped to out-perform them for limited resources. This is best evidenced by the fact that during the recent severe drought the elephants not only remained in the desert but, together with giraffe and rhino, were better able to cope with the tortured conditions than other large mammals. As far as Slang Viljoen was able to ascertain no prime adult desert elephant died as a direct result of the drought, whereas there was a sharp decline in the numbers of kudu, springbok, gemsbok and mountain zebra.

Elephants are able to survive in the northern Namib Desert because, in a sense, they are not solely reliant on what the desert provides in the way of food. Because of the poor and erratic rainfall in the desert, plant growth is very low, unpredictable and – except during brief wet spells – of poor quality. Further to the east, however, annual rainfall increases and the run-off from the rains in the eastern escarpment areas is considerable. This water percolates under the sands of dry riverbeds and gives rise to relatively prolific riparian vegetation, thus creating narrow linear oases which transect the desert from east to west. These watercourses constitute a favourable micro-environment within the desert ecosystem that elephants and many other species are able to exploit. During the long dry season elephants concentrate in the river courses which provide shade, food and water. They help maintain waterholes by excavating the sand in the dry riverbeds, digging down to make neat holes into which the water seeps. When the elephants have finished drinking, myriad other creatures use the same holes. During the drought, elephants were the only animals left which were able to dig for water and their presence frequently meant the difference between life and death for a great number of mammals, birds and insects, dependent on elephant-engineered wells.

Elephants, with their tree-splitting and path-making propensities, have it within their capabilities to modify their habitat radically. In Africa they probably rank only behind man and fire as the greatest force for habitat change, and in parks where elephant numbers have become excessive their impact on the environment can be awesome. So just what effect are such gargantuan herbivores having on the desert's relatively fragile ecological balance? Are they demolition agents, as has been claimed, wreaking irreparable damage on rare endemic plants and the magnificent winter thorns? Finding answers to these questions was one of Slang Viljoen's highest priorities. To do so he carried out a series of intensive plant surveys, concentrated on the dry season habitat types – primarily along the river courses – on which the region's elephant-carrying capacity depends.

The most time-consuming and ultimately the most important daily activity of an elephant is eating. They select from a wide variety of plants, eating some only at certain times of the year or at certain growth stages. They are bulk-feeders and, as they digest only about forty percent of what they eat, it takes a fair amount of vegetation passing through the vast cavern of an elephant's stomach to keep it going – over a hundred kilograms per day for an adult bull. Viljoen found that during the rainy season the elephants' diet consists mainly of nutritious growing grasses. As the grass withers it becomes more fibrous, and at this time of the year the elephants switched back to the higher protein woody plants. Of these, their staples are plants that occur in higher frequencies such as mopane, the winter thorns (*Acacia albida*) and commiphoras – the exceptions being unpalatable species such as the mustard tree (*Salvadora persica*) and wild ebony (*Euclea pseudebenus*). During the drought practically all plant types were used to some extent. Elephants even stripped the desiccated leaf tissue and thick leathery leaves of the endemic welwitchias, but with the return of the rains the stunted leaves began growing again and it was found that none had been killed, as was originally feared.

Elephants seek out certain foods for their mineral content and for a time during the year the desert elephants are very partial to tree bark, perhaps for its high level of calcium. Stripping the bark off trees lets in bacteria, woodborers and diverse other afflictions while ring-barking kills the tree altogether. Concern has been expressed that the magnificent *Acacia albida* are being de-barked at a rate that threatens their existence. Viljoen found that in the Hoanib River, where the largest concentration of elephants occurs, 14 percent of the total amount of winter thorns were dead. Of these 18 percent had been killed by elephants, mostly by ring-barking them, while the rest had died as a result of either floodwaters or fire. However he found that 26 percent of all winter thorns consisted of established young trees. In other words their rate of regeneration more than compensated for the rate of attrition. By comparing aerial photographs taken in 1963 and 1982 and counting the number of trees per hectare, the difference was found to be negligible. His research had shown that for at least the last twenty years there is no sign that the elephants have been destroying one of the region's most important shade and food trees.

On the other hand, in season, the elephants consume great quantities of acacia seed pods which pass through their digestive system – a process that softens the seed's hard testa thereby greatly facilitating their germination. The seeds are then deposited in an immense warm nutritious pile of dung – a most auspicious start in life. When the rains come the seeds in the elephant dung are ready to germinate immediately and so get the full advantage of the rain as opposed to seeds in the pods, which must weather for a long period before the water is able to penetrate the hard testa. Tests have shown that seeds in elephant dung have a germination success rate as high as 75 percent whereas seeds taken from the pod achieve only 12 percent. So quite unwittingly the elephants play an important role in replacing the trees they destroy.

To take a closer look at these desert elephants, I could think of no better way than to

Right: *Dust bathing – elephants kick aside rocks to create dust wallows*

follow them on foot under the same sun. If I was to spend any time in their company I had very little choice – they have no use for mankind and stampede in panic on hearing a vehicle. But by remaining downwind and taking advantage of their myopia I found I could approach to within a hundred metres, even in the absence of cover, without them detecting me.

The best place to look for elephants in the dry season is along the river courses. Each morning I would set out from Wêreldsend in an old Land Rover, picking my way down a rude track that wound through curved slopes of brick-red basalt slashed by mopane-green drainage lines. At this time of year the mopane is particularly important forage for northern Damaraland's elephant populations, because although the trees are deciduous they never completely lose their leaves, except in the wake of frost. In other parts of Africa the highest elephant densities occur where rainfall is between 1400 and 1800mm per annum. Higher rainfall facilitates higher primary productivity and the greater the plant mass the more food available for elephants, so the more of them there will be. In the northern Namib, which receives less than 150mm per year, elephant density averages out at one animal per one hundred square kilometres. With so few elephants left in the desert, finding them can never be taken for granted. But at the height of winter the mopanes are a great attraction and I found the elusive nomads satisfyingly concentrated. Hardly a day went by that I did not encounter at least one herd.

Because of the sparse, bare nature of the country I invariably spotted an elephant before it became aware of the vehicle. My first reaction was to switch off the engine and then assess the situation – wind direction, the direction in which the elephants were feeding and where best to intercept them. Having made my calculations, I would shoulder my camera satchel and tripod then circle around to come up with the herd. I worked hard at preventing them from getting my scent – not only would their flight thwart my objectives but good manners dictated that if I wished to share the elephants' space I should do so without disturbing them. In this way I was able to immerse myself in elephant days, content in their society as they attended to their elephantine affairs.

Although the condensed elephant clans are concentrated along the river courses during the long dry season they are not restricted to them. In contrast to elephants in higher rainfall areas, they need to drink only once every four days, an adaption to their harsh environment that permits them to forage as much as eighty kilometres from the nearest waterhole. One crisp July morning I tagged along behind seven cows and sub-adults as they traversed millennia-old paths across a red laval moonscape of craters, ridges and violently upflung mountains. The primeval forces that shaped the earth had here turned its crust into one huge scar. The bruised land reeled under the raw blast of the sun and the elephants moving across it looked, in the bleached white light, like the last survivors of a Pleistocene holocaust.

The elephants fed desultorily as they slowly forged ahead, casually overturning dwarf commiphoras to get at the roots. Although they were a breeding herd there were no calves amongst them and during my stay in the northern Namib I never saw a calf younger than four years old. In this thirstland, elephant births usually only take place during the cursory rainy season when sprouting vegetation means improved nutrition.

With particularly good rains fertility goes up but during the recent drought – either because oestrus cycles were disrupted or because of a lower conception rate – very few calves were born. Of those that were born during the five years of drought only an average of one per year managed to survive. Once a calf reaches the age of six, however, its chances of survival are good, even under the toughest conditions. In the wake of the previous year's reasonable rains there was every likelihood that the breeding cows in the group were already pregnant, and that after a twenty-two month gestation period, they would once again produce healthy offspring.

In the glare of high noon the elephants took their rest on the table-top crest of an elevated plateau. There was no shade at all, but by the amount of dung in the vicinity it was obviously a favourite elephant stopping place. A dry wallow of loose fine-grained soil – a sandy oasis in a sea of rubbled rocks – had been developed earlier by the transient herds. The elephants clustered together, chipping at the ground with their forefeet, then, taking up the accumulated dust in their trunks, they blew it over themselves, momentarily shrouding the group in a pink talcum curtain that wafted away on the breeze. A coating of dust may help provide the thermal shield against solar radiation that their naked skin does not have. In coping with heat stress elephants resort to a variety of stratagems. No doubt they had come to this high-up promontory for their midday siesta, so as to take full advantage of the convective cooling effect of the south-westerlies that blow off the surface of the Atlantic's icy Benguela Current.

Once the dusting was done, the elephants appeared to doze off – through binoculars it looked as if their eyes were partially closed. But even in repose the herd flowed in perpetual motion – their ears, like delicate great petals, rhythmically fanning with the dry rustle of billowing sails. The motion cools the blood passing through the ears' network of protuberant blood vessels by as much as 6°C, and as the total blood supply may pass through the ears every few minutes, a constant flow of cooled blood is kept circulating throughout the elephant's body. Two of the younger animals put their trunks into their mouths to draw water from their stomachs which they then sprayed behind their ears. I had heard of this practice though had never before seen it, but then anyone who spends sufficient time in elephant company will sooner or later see them do something very strange or out of the ordinary. Within their limitations they show a remarkable capacity for resource and resilience.

The elephants stood stolid and stiff-legged, except when they wished to relieve the pressure on their soles, when they would prop a foot up on to its toenails or jauntily cross their back legs. They were totally at ease and sitting amongst them I felt transported back many centuries to a time when man was part of the animal world – an animal among others. There was a great stillness; in the absence of all other sound, the *whoosh* of the elephants' ears, and the occasional rough chafing as two flanks rubbed, carried on the dry air and was magnified. I gazed about at the vast wilderness all around; no sign of man, no mark or sound for hundreds of kilometres. This land has never been settled. At best it was put to seasonal use by nomadic pastoralists and hunter-gatherers who left little enough evidence of their passing. It was once part of the Etosha Game Reserve and is today still too arid to support year-round ranching.

To exist in these western badlands the elephants, like other successful desert animals, have evolved a multiplicity of adaptations, the concerted effect of which is to conserve water and energy reserves. Although there has been speculation that the elephants have made physiological adaptions as well as behavioural, there is no evidence to support this. Taxonomically they are not likely to differ from elephants in other parts of Africa and cannot be described as a subspecies. However they have developed the ability to survive conditions of low food availability and long intervals between drinking; they are able to cover long distances in search of forage and water and take opportunistic advantage of the erratic rainfall. In an arid area, water and energy budgets are critical. Desert elephants do not waste energy, they cannot afford to – they go straight to food and water. In order to do so they must have an intimate knowledge of their home range, a knowledge that permits them to take the most convenient route, across a bare gravel plain, to a waterhole that may be sixty kilometres from the nearest neighbouring water. Their navigation must be unerring – if they miss it, they could die.

As Slang Viljoen has pointed out, the possibility that the desert elephants represent a new, unique ecotype or subspecies is not the main criterion when considering their conservation. What is important is the unique combination of the animals and their environment and that they comprise an ecological population that is irreplaceable.

It is not always clear which aspects of an animal's behaviour are innate and which are learned, but field studies have revealed that a good deal of elephant behaviour is learned or acquired. A calf stays with its mother for up to ten years, a long childhood second only to man's. It grows up in the company of other elephants of varying ages, accumulating knowledge on how to make a living in its environment, such as which plants are palatable and which parts of the plant to eat. While moving about with the herd, the calf also learns the secrets of its home range – where there is water, when different plants come into season and where they can be found, where to go for relief in the heat of the day and how to avoid its only predator – hunting man. In times of drought, an elephant's memory and experience may be the key to survival. The desert elephants thrive in the desert because they have grown up in it, are privy to its intricacies. To suggest, as has been done, that should they ever be hunted into oblivion they could, at some time in the future, be replaced by surplus elephants translocated from Etosha, is to ignore biological lore and past experience. The few attempts that have been made to relocate wild elephants mechanically have shown that only young animals could be moved, at enormous cost and ultimately with limited success. As juveniles would have no hope of surviving alone in the desert, whole family groups would have to be housed in special crates, loaded by cranes onto heavy-duty lorries and transported over great distances on poor roads at astronomical expense. With the outcome of such a project dubious from the start, it is highly unlikely that it would ever be implemented. Ironically, the people promoting the idea do not envisage the translocation of elephants as a means of supplementing the indigenous desert population but as an alternative to conserving it. That approach is impractical and in all probability unlikely and the rationale behind it is as insidious as it is wrong-headed.

The desert elephants have already been eradicated from much of their former range. One of their last strongholds is the Hoanib River, where some twenty cows and subadults and about six bulls live a precarious existence. Wandering elephants still

Right: *Elephants in the Hoanib riverbed*

occasionally range as far east as Khowarib, where the Hoanib cuts through stark towering limestone mountains to form a canyon flanked by precipitous cliffs. It is rugged beautiful country – harmonious and remorseless and utterly imcomparable. Only a decade ago, elephant herds regularly patronized the spring that rises close to where the Hoanib emerges from the gorge. To have seen elephants here was to have seen them in one of the most spectacular settings in Africa.

On my first visit to the western reaches of the Hoanib, Garth brought me to a disintegrating elephant skeleton that floodwaters had not yet flushed away. It had been gunned down a year before. All that remained of that once vital life force was a cracked hollow-eyed skull, the splintered staves of its ribs, bleached knuckles and scraps of petrified hide. There was nothing to be said; in the ringing dread silence that stalks wild places from which all the wild animals have gone, we were both of us left alone with our thoughts.

Retreating still further westwards, we came to where the Ganamub River joins the Hoanib, and here, for the first time, we encountered live elephants. A mature bull, with small tusks, had joined two adult cows and an eight year old subadult bull in hiding-out in a low salvadora thicket. It has become the custom of the Hoanib elephants to withdraw into cover on hearing the clatter of an approaching vehicle and to remain out of sight until the intruders have passed.

We abandoned the Land Rover and worked our way to the river bank on foot, where an elevated ledge gave us an uninterrupted view. The elephants had gathered into a tight defensive circle, the young bull towards the centre. A grey lourie brayed an alarm call and the elephants fidgeted uneasily. At intervals one or the other would cast a trunkful of dust over its back. The broad salvadora-choked bed of the river looked like a shallow valley or an amphitheatre, encircled by dark looming fortress mountains. It would photograph well; the scene was strikingly composed, the colours in dramatic counterpoint. But what it portrayed was less than it concealed. What a photograph would miss was the palpable sense of fear that the elephants radiated, the aura of tragedy and waste as the great fragile beasts made a bewildered last stand.

The brooding elephants, tense with expectation, with the apprehended presence of man, were diminished by the sweep and grandeur of their surroundings; they looked like miniature figurines in an improbable garden. The wild country, the doomed animals were of another age and I felt daunted by the might and the vulnerability of the old continent. Then the turgid breeze shifted and the elephants scented us. One of them trumpeted, splitting the air with a scream summoned up from prehistory and they broke from cover with a pounding, heavy gait. They surged down the riverbed, bursting through shrubbery without breaking stride. Around a bend in the river they disappeared from sight, tiny in the distance, but still running hard.

CHAPTER

# 4

# Walking the Red Plains

To know the essence of wild country one needs to walk it; this is probably more true of deserts than of any other type of terrain. It is only on foot, under a blue emptiness of sky, that the intrinsic nature of the desert, its almost unrelenting hostility, reveals itself. Walking the red plains in the vicinity of Wêreldsend, I could empathise with the great herbivores I had seen trudging across wind-weathered stones, through a vast shimmering vacuity that unravelled without sign of another bird or beast. Out there it was easy to imagine that I had come to a place at the end of the world, to a place that denied hope or possibility. I thought of a lone elephant bull I had seen determinedly plodding across just such a plain as this. I knew now, absolutely, what I had suspected then – that he was hurrying through a no-man's-land, from one point to another; there was nothing for him out there.

The most discouraging part of walking those plains was, on gaining a rise, to see my objective – a dry riverbed or rocky krantz – ten kilometres away and, through binoculars, see nothing of interest on the exposed, revealed landscape to relieve the hard slog ahead. And the view of the route was deceptive; the hard flat light smoothed out the folds in the land, so country that appeared to be as level as a board became a wearying series of climbs and descents. The tedium was as enervating as the exertion.

The only soft note in that scorched landscape was the voice of an occasional lark. I shared with the wildlife the comfort to be taken in the dry riverbeds, where tall trees provided an escape from the brassy glare and the sun-stunned vistas all around. One afternoon I followed a breeding herd of elephants that I had stayed with all morning, as they set out from the shaded Achab River for a destination only they knew of. They walked with a purposefulness that had me jogging to keep up. A hot wind slapped my face and, weighed down by my camera satchel and tripod, I was soon panting. Flies were sucked into my open mouth and were stifled there. It was very hard work; I was fatigued by the physical strain of running but also by the sun and wind, the dryness. Dehydration was the threat; I sweated fluids that were immediately evaporated and so went unnoticed. While on the move I was hardly aware of expended energy – it was only when I stopped to rest that a wave of exhaustion swept over me. I retraced my steps to the spring and drank until my belly swelled and gurgled with its load, but still I felt the need to take in more.

This lonely arid land would seem to have little to recommend it to a Nordic émigré, and I wondered what had kept the nineteenth century explorer Charles John Anderson here, in a country he described as 'that most repulsive and least accessible quarter of the globe'; a country that had so badly used him, had bankrupted him, ruined his health and ultimately killed him. Perhaps it was, as his publisher suggested, 'the perverseness of human nature' that drove him on. He had started out full of youthful confidence and idealism: 'It was at the close of the year 1849, that I left Gothenburg in a sailing vessel, for Hull,' he opens his journal. 'Though a Swede by birth I am half an Englishman by parentage . . . From my earliest youth, my day-dreams had carried me into the wilds of Africa. Passionately fond of travelling, accustomed from my childhood to field sports, and to the study of natural history, and (as I hope I may say with truth) desirous of rendering myself useful in my generation, I earnestly longed to explore some portion of that continent where all my predilections could be fully indulged.'

On arriving at 'Walfisch Bay' (Walvisbay) however, the reality of the situation impressed itself upon him. 'The first appearance of the coast,' he reported, 'is little calculated to inspire confidence in the traveller about to penetrate into the interior. A desert of sand . . . I thought it the most dismal spot that human eye ever rested on. But, in the short space of a few weeks, it had almost become endeared to me. I found what Shakespeare calls the "soul of goodness in things evil". Dreariness was softened down into peaceful seclusion; the savage country round about assumed the dignity of primeval nature, fresh from the hand of the Creator; and the solemn and stern night-silence only hushed me into sounder sleep.'

Anderson adjusted remarkably quickly to his new circumstances. To condition and toughen himself, 'when he first arrived in Africa, he generally travelled on foot throughout the whole of the day, regardless of heat, and almost scorning the idea of riding on horseback, or using any other mode of conveyance.' The Damaraland he penetrated was at the time uncharted by Europeans, and Anderson assiduously collected, cartographed, quantified and reported back to science and the general public through geographical societies and the popular press. He approvingly noted that, 'Africa may be said, even up to the present day, to be principally inhabited by wild beasts'. He dismissed the Africans he encountered in the peremptory tones of colonial contempt. 'Its savage human natives only afford a study of rational life on so low a scale as hardly to justify the epithet I have just made use of; whereas one may, in the regions I have frequented, luxuriate in the contemplation of pure animal existence in its fullest and freest developments. In brief, Africa is a vast zoological garden, and a vast hunting field at the same time.'

Anderson was a strong man, strong-minded and strong-willed; his enemies were the elements, the country itself, and he fought them all the way, but there, in Damaraland, the earth seemed unearthly . . . 'sandhills, miles and miles in extent, rising several hundred feet in altitude, and changing their terror-inspiring aspect with every fresh and strong wind that blows; there a naked granite rock or boulder, reflecting from its reddish-looking surface a glaring and insupportable heat; or huge heaps of black ironstone, neighbouring perhaps a dazzling white limestone ridge, all destitute of vegetation. This is its appearance; and there are hundreds of miles along the west coast, northwards and southwards – even extending far inland – precisely like it. Indeed it might vie with the Great Sahara itself in sterility and dreariness; and the weary eye seems to range in vain over this howling wilderness, in search of some object worthy of attention.'

The cruel, constant struggles wore Anderson down; increasingly he gave way to the morbid melancholic disposition that inhabits the souls of many of his north European countrymen: 'During the long and sleepless nights I was often seized with an indescribable sensation of sadness and melancholy. Death itself I did not fear; but to perish in a foreign land, in the midst of strangers, far away from all I loved, was an idea to which I could hardly reconcile myself. What hand would close my eyes? What mourner would follow my coffin? Or what friend would shed a tear on my lonely and distant grave? I was *alone*!'

The severe hardships Anderson underwent, his trials and privations, seem to have catered to a subliminal masochistic streak in his nature – the harder the going, the more determined he become to push on, often in the face of common sense and good advice. In the end, he died much as he had dreaded he would, alone except for his young assistant Axel Erikson, while attempting to reach the Kunene River in spite of his steadily deteriorating health. He died in despair, at the age of forty, probably from a perforated duodenal ulcer. At the time he was insolvent to the point where his family in Cape Town were forced to rely on charity; his one leg had been crippled by a bullet during a past skirmish with a band of Namas and his general constitution had been debilitated by fevers and other maladies contracted during his African wanderings. Yet it is very likely this zealotry, this willingness to make any sacrifice to achieve a stated goal – more so than courage – that best defines the character and qualities of the great explorers. Nor had Anderson's sufferings been in vain – his carefully recorded observations were of great importance in furthering the knowledge of the natural sciences in a country which had up till then been little more than a blank space on a map.

Looking back, it is almost impossible to comprehend the adversities that had confronted Anderson, even though Damaraland is still today very harsh country. He had challenged the unknown; the danger had been the invasion of a *terra incognita* without recourse to any support systems. I was thinking of Anderson's lament – 'I had penetrated into deserts almost unknown to civilized man; had suffered the extremity of hunger and thirst, cold and heat; and had undergone desperate toil, sometimes nearly in solitude, and often without shelter during dreary nights in vast wildernesses, haunted by beasts of prey' – when I accompanied a group of visitors that Garth was guiding on a day trip from Windhoek through the stony deserts to the west of Wêreldsend. The visitors' enthusiastic chatter buoyed them up, armoured them against the desolation. They were appreciative of the sweep of the country, charmed by its bleakness. They applied suntan lotion, offered oranges. What was next on the agenda? That evening back at camp they would talk about what they had seen today over cold drinks, after hot showers. They would have opinions, make suggestions, recall the day's highlights without ever realising that the wilderness they had toured was the same place but an altogether different world to the one Anderson had entered.

On my walks I learned soon enough to hold to the dry river courses as far as possible. Not only was the going easier but it was more interesting as, like myself, most of the wildlife in the district favoured these retreats. Once, in the riverbed's firm sand I saw the deeply scored tracks of a fleeing kudu overlaid by those of a pursuing hyena. Although I would never discover the outcome of that chase, I was later told that here kudus are a favourite prey of the coursing, remorseless spotted hyena.

That night, at Wêreldsend, I heard a hyena for the first time. It's weird ululations carried from afar on the still night air, indistinct but unmistakable. It was a reassuring and happy sound; and whether proclaiming occupation of its territory or seeking companionship, it was resuming an age-old custom that had been disrupted when human persecution made advertising its presence a hazardous proposition.

It might have been the same hyena that, a few days later, I watched from a tent-hide I had erected amongst the sedge bordering a seep, as it loped in from across the bare plains, in an early morning light, for a drink. A pair of resident jackals reacted suspiciously to the hyena's approach, although it paid them no heed. Making strange little grunts, one of the jackals shiftily edged up behind the hyena as if he had it in mind to snap at its heels but when the hyena swung its big angular head in the jackal's direction the little canine nearly fell over itself to get out of the way. Perhaps the jackal was only being mischievous, for later in the morning, for no discernible reason, it challenged a family of springbok and again had to scramble for safety when an incensed ewe lunged at it.

Soon after first light thirsty doves arrived on singing wings, in their grey-feathered legions. Among them, swirling flocks of dull brown lark-like buntings looked like untidy blown scraps that broke apart and boiled up when a lanner falcon swept by overhead. By mid-morning the air was full of the high fluted whispers of converging Namaqua sandgrouse, easily the most characteristic sound of southern Africa's thirstlands. Triggered by the recuperative rains of the previous year, the sandgrouse had embarked on a continuous breeding cycle, which in the desert is nature's way of compensating for the losses incurred during the bad times. Two or three eggs are laid in a hollow scraped in the ground; soon after hatching the precocious chicks leave the nest and, unable to fly for the first three weeks, waddle after their parents as they search for hard seeds. The young birds are cryptically patterned with brown and white flecks that match the substrate, be it rock or scattered pebbles, almost perfectly. If danger threatens they go to earth, relying on their camouflage colouration to make them visually undetectable to a predator. Quite frequently on my walks I came across chicks crouched silent and unmoving, while the adults withdrew to anxiously watch over them from a safe distance.

All along the riverbeds I constantly encountered the twin furrows that a rhino makes by kicking backwards to scatter its dung, as well as squirts of their urine – which in this arid environment is remarkably viscous so as to enhance fluid retention – pasted on to boulders. On the open gravel plains there were many *Euphorbia damarana* with their fronds flattened into mattresses by rhinos seeking comfort and shade for their midday siestas. I imagined rounding one of those bushes to find myself face to face with a rhino at rest on its nest, like a warm-blooded latter-day pterodactyl, and very displeased at being disturbed. But though their signs were everywhere, the animals themselves remained tantalisingly elusive, and I always counted myself lucky whenever I saw one.

Right: *A mating pair of armoured ground crickets – the male attracts the female by rubbing his wing stumps to produce a loud note*

Most of the rhinos in Damaraland and Kaokoland have been documented and named by Garth Owen-Smith and others; so I could compare a description of any animal I sighted with those already on record. There was, for instance, the Carcabin cow – so named because she was first seen near a spring with the shell of an abandoned car lying alongside it. She had a reputation for truculence and looked very old and wrinkled, with big plates of skin hanging from her flanks, reminiscent of an Asian rhino. She was instantly recognisable by a short hooked anterior horn that had regrown after breaking off and by her tail that had lost the tuft at its tip and instead ended in a piggish curl. The old girl was known to wander over a huge range, and where I came across her she was eighty kilometres from the Carcabin Spring. I came to know the Mudorib cow and her infant calf; and Pinocchio, a massive bull whose name celebrated his awesome forward-jutting horn.

One morning, shortly after sun-up, I came upon a young rhino cow and managed to stay with her until the sun dropped behind a mountain that evening. She was an attractive animal, as rhinos go, with a curved, sharply defined though not exceptionally large anterior horn and a pert posterior horn. Her ears were without tears or holes and prettily fringed, the bristles trapping the late afternoon backlight in a gingerish halo above her head. She looked in sleek good condition and bore no distinguishing nicks or scars.

Little is known about how desert rhinos cope in their rugged environment and I valued this opportunity to observe the cow from downwind as she attended to what I imagined to be a typical day's activities. I surreptitiously followed her as she crossed a broad laval plain; she made heavy going of it over the basalt boulders, moving with a clatter and occasionally stumbling. She was feeding as she forged ahead but whenever feasible she held to a well-used path from which the rocks had been kicked aside, as did I.

Once she stopped to investigate a sandy space that was used as a rhino dunging midden, and which was covered with the scattered, desiccated, faecal signposting that proclaims an animal's presence in its home range. In response, the cow swivelled round and herself defecated on the spot, kicking back desultorily with her hind foot without disturbing the pile. No sooner had she moved on than a mountain chat flew over to rummage through the coarse droppings for undigested morsels.

From the little evidence to hand, it would appear that desert rhinos are remarkably well adapted to their hostile habitat, even more so than the other large herbivores, as they are not dependent on the dry river courses for food. Rhinos browse on almost all of the approximately 350 different plants that occur in their desert homeland, including the *Euphorbia damarana* which is poisonous to man. The cow I was trailing used her long prehensile top lip to pluck delicately the small, round, yellow-ripe fruits of a euphorbia and then went on to chew the succulent tips of the smooth, slender branchlets, extracting the copious flow of milky latex and leaving the shredded tips drooping like a tassle. During exceptionally dry periods this species of euphorbia provides an important source of moisture when waterholes are few and far between. That its toxic latex can be ingested without ill effect is little short of astonishing, as the substance is so corrosive that whenever kudu feed off the bush and the latex drips on to their coats, it scorches the hair off. I had been using euphorbias – the only vegetation of any size in the area – to screen myself from the rhino and in so doing had got latex on myself and my camera equipment. As a result I had to be careful how I went about relieving facial itches, bearing in mind what had happened to Garth when latex had dried on his hand; giving it no further thought, he later wiped his brow and in so doing had rubbed the poison into his eye, provoking excruciating pain.

Every so often the cow would loft her tail to squirt small quantities of urine, an action that almost certainly indicated she was on heat. The urine's hormone content would alert any bull that sniffed at it as to the cow's condition and, responding to her scent, he would then doggedly seek her out. As a means to facilitate breeding in an unsociable species that lives widely dispersed, urine squirting is very efficient advertising, but I wondered what effect it was having on the cow's water reserves. My wondering was answered when, towards noon, she walked into a dense patch of shrubs and proceeded to drink from a tiny secret pool I would never have guessed was there.

The sight of her drinking was a revelation; she held her head high after each sip and flared her top lip, the overspill dribbling to the ground. From where I sat I could clearly hear her gurgling swallows. Desert rhinos are not only able to make best use of the water they take in, but also know of many more sources than we do. Moreover, rhinos are known to seek out certain plants at certain times of the drought or rain cycle, and the late John Goddard found that, in the more arid regions of the Olduvai Gorge in Tanzania, some rhinos did not drink at all in the dry season. They stuck to their small home ranges even after all the waterholes dried up and there was no indication that they walked long distances to the nearest water. They did however concentrate their feeding on succulent plants and those with a high moisture content, and Goddard postulated that the rhinos could survive on the juices from these moisture-rich plants alone.

During the hot midday hours the cow took her siesta, first on a bed of euphorbia fronds and then in a sand wallow surrounded by a field of rocks, while I waited in the shade of a shepherd's tree, comfortably sprawled against boulders that had been spattered white by generations of roosting birds. The only disturbance was the attention paid me by tough rubbery horseflies that came armed with a bad bite. They were slow moving but impervious to slaps, and the recommended method of dispatching them was to grip them between the thumb and index finger of one hand, tweaking off their heads with the other.

The cow lay on her brisket, legs curled under her. Every so often she would rise to stretch cramped muscles, expressing her relaxation with wide yawns that lent her an endearing air of bemused innocence. Her vulnerability was all that a poacher could ask for and the northern Namib's rhino population has been decimated because of a notion among Orientals that rhino 'horn' – really nothing more than compacted hair and gelatin – is a cure for everything from headaches to carbuncles to demonic possession. An infusion of their shavings is also lauded in some quarters as a powerful aphrodisiac – a belief that, in spite of the horn's dynamic shape and angle, has absolutely no basis in reality. Which is, as one naturalist observed, the ultimate outrage, as the horns are of no use to anyone but the rhinos themselves. Yet today that worthless commodity fetches a higher price than pure gold.

I could imagine nothing more alien than the roar of a rifle in that vast and harmonious silence. It would have been a savage, grotesque desecration. Propped against the bole of a tree with the big primitive pachyderm only a few metres away and every horizon bounded by a broken, pristine desert kingdom, I experienced great peace of mind.

Here all forms of animal life were sparse, but that was in keeping with the nature of the country. While trailing the rhino I had seen a yellow snake slither – too quickly to identify – from its place in the sun to the shelter of a dwarf commiphora. Small brown geckoes drifted between the rocks. During the course of the day, flights of lark-like buntings had passed, as had individual sparrows, chirping unmusically. A family group of Rüppell's bustards went on their way, their exchanges sounding like a weird variation on a frog's croak, and a party of Ludwig's bustards in heavy, strong flight. The only other mammals I saw were a kudu cow and calf that cantered close past, although in 1972 the ecologist Ken Tinley had counted, in this same Uniab catchment, 1000 mountain zebra and 2000 springbok that had gathered to take advantage of fresh grass growth in the wake of a localised shower.

In the late afternoon the cow resumed browsing, moving from one desiccated but obviously highly favoured *Maerua* creeper to the next, on a direct line to where I was standing behind my tripod, alongside a tree. At first she reacted to the click of the camera with little starts of alarm and once raised dust with a short mock charge but she surprisingly quickly came to accept the unfamiliar sound and kept right on coming towards me. Before long she had ambled to within fifteen metres – I later stepped it out – the closest I have ever been to a rhino on foot. I had not wanted to retreat before her as I had reasoned that any movement would catch her attention and anyway the shepherd's tree under which I stood was the only shelter anywhere around. It suddenly occurred to me that it was the tree that the rhino was heading for and wanting to get out of harm's way I started to scramble into the low branches. This burst of noise and activity galvanised the rhino. For a moment she could have gone either way – charge or retreat – I was far too close, deep in her space, but then she turned, nervous as I was, and trotted away with her tail curled tightly over her back.

'The Kaoko and Damaraland rhinos seem less apt to charge than those in East Africa,' the German hunter Wilhelm Steinhardt commented after a visit to the territory in the early part of this century, 'and are usually content to give chase for a short distance only.' How true that opinion is, is open to speculation. It does seem to be generally true that dominant bulls are more likely to charge with serious intent than cows are, but the unpredictability of the beast's temper is guaranteed, sooner or later, to make nonsense of any hard-and-fast rule.

To this day I am not sure what to make of an encounter Garth and I had with a cow we came upon near the Uniab River. She was shuffling along, peacefully browsing ground-level plants that erupted between the rocks of an otherwise naked surface. The click of my camera alerted her – she pricked her ears and stared with myopic tension towards us. We were close enough for her to see us silhouetted against the horizon, without her being able to define what it was she was seeing. Another click, curiosity and insupportable suspicion fully aroused, the rhino started towards us. 'She's coming,' Garth said quietly. 'I'll keep photographing until you say

Right: *Female desert rhino charging author*

run,' I replied. I was relying on our making our escape down the steep river bank behind us – too steep, I felt sure, for a rhino to follow. Anyway, after all the time I had spent simply *looking* for a rhino to photograph, this was too good an opportunity to let pass.

I tripped the shutter again and the cow charged. In one fluid motion Garth stooped, grabbed a rock and threw it at the oncoming rhino. His aim was either immaculate or very lucky – the missile bounced off the cow's snout and the shock of the impact stopped her in her tracks, then she whirled and barrelled off, fleeing without breaking stride until she disappeared from sight in the Uniab's close riverine vegetation.

It had been a heart-stopping experience and one which, I suppose, could have very easily gone out of control. Certainly Elias, who had been watching the proceedings from a little way off, thought so. He was deeply offended by what he regarded as our reckless behaviour. 'You play with the rhino,' he scolded with barely contained fury, 'but the rhino doesn't know that and one day when he catches you he won't be playing.' I could think of nothing to say to refute the censure in his argument. It is generally true that people, be they black or white, who have grown up among wild animals prefer not to take chances, and bravado is held in very low regard. They know from experience how quickly and easily things can go wrong.

Just how easily was illustrated by a clash between a party of Nama hunters and a desert rhino that took place in 1837, later recounted by the gentleman-explorer Sir James Edward Alexander in his resonant *Expedition of Discovery into the Interior of Africa*:

They crossed the fresh track of a rhinoceros, and shortly afterwards saw a large black male in a bush. Henrick immediately 'becrept' him, and with his long elephant rifle he inflicted a severe wound on his foreleg. The rhinoceros charged, the men fled, and the monster singling one of them out, closely pursued him, when the man stopping short, whilst the horn of the rhinoceros was ploughing up the ground at his heels, and dexterously jumping to one side, the rhinoceros missed him and passed in full career, and before the brute could recover himself and change his course, the whole of the party had got up into trees, whilst the limping rhinoceros was trying in vain to hunt them out by smell. One of the men, named Arasap, and armed with an assegai, said to his comrades, 'Why are we all doing nothing? Shoot! Shoot!'

'Well,' said Henrick, 'if you are in a hurry to shoot without waiting for the proper time, here is my powder-horn and ball-belt for you, and my gun is at the bottom of the tree.'

Accordingly, Arasap descended from his tree, loaded the gun, and approaching the rhinoceros, he fired and wounded him severely but not mortally in the jaw; the ball was a leaden one, it did not break the bone, but was flattened against it, and stunned and dropped the animal.

The hunters now collected round the rhinoceros, thinking that it was incapable of rising again; and Arasap, in the pride of his heart, was directing the rest how to stab him with the best effect with their assegais in different parts, when the beast, beginning to recover, spurtled or kicked with his legs, and Henrick calling to the men to run for their lives, he set them the example, and swift footed like Camilla, he scoured the plain, and was soon out of danger. The rhinoceros started up, singled out the unfortunate Arasap, and with ears erect, and screaming and snorting with rage, he thundered after him. Arasap, seeing that he was unable to outrun him, tried the same trick with which the other hunter had succeeded; that is, he stopped short, and hoped that the rhinoceros would pass him; the brute was not to be baulked a second time, but catching the doomed man on his horn under the left thigh (which was cut open as if an axe had been used) he tossed him a dozen yards into the air!

Arasap fell facing the rhinoceros, and with his legs spread; the beast rushed at him, ripped up his abdomen to the ball-belt, and again threw him aloft. Henrick looked around, and saw Arasap like a jacket in the air. He fell heavily on the ground; the rhinoceros watched his fall, and running up to him, he trod upon him and pounded him to death. Arasap expired with the Namaqua exclamation of surprise and fear on his lips, 'Eisey! Eisey!'

The hunters later destroyed the rhino and, throughout the country, indeed over the entire southern subcontinent, that wave of destruction continued unabated until almost all of the great grey animals were dead. In the past they were as likely to be slain for their flesh as for their horns and Alexander noted that 'after partaking of rhinoceros soup I was much stronger in walking and running than at other times.' Today, once its profitable prong of compacted erect hair has been hacked off, the carcass is left to rot under the hot sun.

One March morning in 1983, Garth and his assistant Peter Erb, acting on a tip-off that suspicious human tracks had been seen in one of the main 'problem' areas, set off on a foot patrol and literally bumped into a small rhino calf wandering alone. The hapless little creature was being harried by three jackals that had already lacerated its ears, forehead and groin. As rhino calves are dependent on their mothers for protection from predators and never naturally leave their sides, the two men immediately realized that something was amiss. While Garth remained with the calf to prevent it from being further attacked by jackals, Peter returned to Wêreldsend to radio the conservation authorities.

With their arrival, a careful reconnoitre revealed the freshly-killed carcass of the little calf's mother. She had been shot to death, and her horns removed. If Garth and Peter had not happened on the scene when they did, the calf – probably ignored by the poachers, its bump of a horn not making it worth the trouble to kill – would have succumbed to the jackals or at best lingered on till evening when the whoop of the hyena summoned the night feeders. As it was, the bewildered orphan was rescued and treated for its wounds. For the first few weeks it was bottle-fed at Wêreldsend and quickly became accustomed to the company of humans. Later it was transferred to Etosha, where the loving care and attention given it by the park's vet and his wife ensured that it matured into a healthy and well-adjusted young adult.

Black rhinos are strangely compelling creatures, mysterious and dramatic and, like the leopard, the epitome of wildness. Whether in Etosha, Zululand or here in Damaraland, I have spent more time looking for the fractious hook-lipped rhino than any other species – most of the time on foot – and as often as not my quest has been unsuccessful. On one occasion I joined Garth on a surveillance patrol to look into the welfare of the rhinos living in the Nqabas Valley. 'We named it ourselves,' he told me as we set out. 'It means rhino in Damara but you won't find it on a map. A strong spring rises on the slopes to form a pool on the valley floor and up till a year ago there was a lot of rhino sign about. There are no car tracks going in and I very much doubt if anyone could even bundu-bash their way in – the terrain is simply too rugged. That rules out any motorised poachers but the fellows we have to worry about here are those that operate with donkey-power.'

We made a steep climb up the valley wall along a game trail that was hoof-pocked by mountain zebra, and had recently been negotiated stolidly by a herd of elephants. Now and again we passed circular depressions in the path where zebras had scraped aside rocks to excavate a dust wallow. From the heights, through binoculars, we saw three giraffe gliding with great dignity across the amorphous bottomlands. Abruptly the deep silence was transformed by the pure, sweet song of a serenading bokmakierie, conjuring haunted notes from what sounded like a magic barrel. The bird was as beautiful to behold as it was to hear; its bright yellow throat, encircled by a black gorget, sparkled in the pearly sun. She flew in close to take a better look at us, fidgeted on a bare branch for a moment, then vigorously scratched her chin. 'Displacement activity,' Garth murmured. 'We're making her nervous.' She hopped to the ground and scuttled away over the boulders with the flowing grace of a serpent.

On the mountain crest, where it formed a level ledge, a carpeting of elephant droppings proclaimed that the herd, like ourselves, had stopped here to rest. In the wild blowing light, beneath a high winter sun, Nqabas Valley lay cupped in the foothills of surrounding mountains. No road was visible, nor any sign of man; from up here it looked as if the mighty landscape had hardly changed in millions of years. Although the elephants' eyesight would have been insufficient to have discerned the land below them, I was tempted to think that, 'half-reasoning' as they undoubtedly are, they might have stood here and pondered on their fate as fugitives in the land of their ancestors.

Garth scanned the country through binoculars for a long while, then lowered them with a sigh. 'Not a single rhino, not even a mountain zebra – nothing. What's disturbing is that none of the old rhino middens we passed has been used recently.'

A sudden movement caught my eye and I turned in time to see a magnificent kudu bull slip from cover and bound with astonishing agility across the mountain face, white flared tail folded back over his rump. 'One of the survivors,' Garth mumbled moodily, 'one of the hard core – made it through the drought, he'll pass on good genes.' But he refused to be mollified by his own observation and restlessly made a last sweep with his binoculars, as if willing a rhino to materialise out of the earth.

On our descent into the valley our trail converged with others, until they formed a well-developed track. 'When we first came into this valley,' Garth remarked, 'we found any number of spoor – zebra, rhino, kudu and elephant – headed in this direction. We guessed they must lead to water and followed them up there. It's a perennial pool, you can tell by the type of vegetation it supports.'

The stone pool had the aspect of a haven, lush with sedges, reeds and moss. The water I scooped into my mouth was as clear as the desert wind. Our arrival startled a rare night heron into revealing itself and, from the uppermost branches of a leadwood, a flock of brilliantly coloured rosy-faced lovebirds hurled shrill imprecations at our heads. These little parrots frequent arid country, but are nevertheless very dependent on water, and the sound of their shrieks is a sure indication that a pool is not far away.

Scarlet dragonflies, far removed from their nearest kin, zipped translucent-winged through the dry heat; the web of a yellow-and-red orb spider spanned a miniature crevasse; lark-like buntings whirling in to drink settled all around the motionless men without recognising any danger. An immature African hawkeagle was harried from its perch by a grey hornbill and a rock kestrel acting in concert. The hornbill trailed the

*Right: Springbok ram in reflection of spring water*

hawkeagle the breadth of the valley, whistling all the while in high indignation.

On high ground above the pool were the remains of a poacher's camp and scattered over it were the identifiable bones of a young rhino and a kudu, and a few thoroughly gnawed corn cobs. Garth had found the site on an earlier patrol, and pointed it out to me in a very matter-of-fact way. 'They came in with pack donkeys and stayed for a while; you can see where the donkeys chewed on the bark of the *Boscia* they were tethered to.'

Further down the track we came to an old hunting scherm – a circular wall of boulders with hewn tree trunks serving as a roof, the sturdiness of the blind no doubt designed to withstand an attack from a wounded and incensed elephant or rhino. Judging by the condition of the mopane logs, Garth estimated that the scherm could be as old as fifty years and built at a time when hunting was done with bows and arrows. In those days it was legal for tribesmen to be hunters and was part of their tradition. In stalking elephants they had to get very close so that the arrow could penetrate the thick hide. It was a risky proposition, and armed as they were, they earned whatever fell to their arrow. But now those skills are lost and will never be revived.

A little beyond the scherm we crossed the fresh spoor of a big bull rhino and although time was pressing we took up its trail in the hope of catching sight of it. But the old fellow was moving haphazardly, wandering from the sandy path to select from a variety of shrubs, and when we lost his tracks on a rocky surface we could not assume that by going on we would eventually intercept them again. We gave up the search with the knowledge that at least this one had survived, but always the question – for how much longer?

I saw at first-hand the grievous effects of uncontrolled poaching when I accompanied Chris Eyre to Otjomenye – The Place of the Springbok – in northern Damaraland, to collect the ivory from an elephant carcass spotted during an aerial survey. Driving the gravel Sesfontein road through mopane-studded plains perforated by khaki-coloured buttes, Chris remarked, 'This country must have been full of game in the old days – short annual grass after the rains, zebras love it. Before the introduction of so much domestic stock this area was covered with grass. Apart from cattle and goats, donkeys are now becoming a problem – they don't need so many, four or so to pull a cart, and the rest should be slaughtered. Donkey meat is a great favourite among the Damaras.'

We left the road to follow a rough track as far as a temporary Herero 'post' in the vicinity of Numas Ugams Spring. 'By rights these Herero herders shouldn't be here in Damaraland – they've moved in from Kaokoland,' Chris told me. 'But the Damara authorities are reluctant to do anything about it, they're too unsure of themselves. They remember all too well that not so long ago the Hereros had the power of life and death over them and although now the two tribes are theoretically equal, the Damaras haven't quite convinced themselves of that fact yet. For that matter, nor have the Hereros.'

After the formal greetings had been disposed of, Chris made a short speech warning against poaching and asked if any game had been seen in the district. The herdsmen spoke of a few ostriches, an occasional springbok and steenbok – very little – although later we were to come across fresh zebra spoor.

We set off with Chris's assistant, Lucas Mpomporo in the lead, his terrier Fergie racing alongside, then dashing off into a thicket, anxious to investigate everything. Fergie's *joie de vivre* was so irrepressible that even when he picked up thorns he carried on hopping at full speed, first on three legs then on two. Finally, when thorns became imbedded in a third foot, he would sit for a moment, gnaw furiously at his pad, then be up and off again. For no apparent reason he would sometimes attack trees; leaping at a supple branch until he caught it between his teeth, he would hang suspended in the air and, growling and whining, would worry and shake the branch fiercely until it broke or he had to let go in order to catch up with us.

Every so often Chris would admonish him with affectionate indulgence, 'Calm down, Fergie, you're going to tire yourself out.' At which Fergie, panting and long tongue lolling, would stop and stare up at Chris, then, satisfied the command could be safely ignored, would dash away as before. 'Fergie's heart is bigger than his brain,' Chris said, watching his dog's nutty antics. 'He keeps going until he's too exhausted to move. I've ended up having to carry him home on more than one occasion.'

It was a lovely day for walking, warm crisp winter sunshine, but in the coppery air there was a sense of foreboding. We were passing through what should have been prime game country, but the only sign of vertebrate life was a lone mountain chat that alighted on a squat-boled pachypodium thrust up from the rocky crest of a hill like a tombstone; and the chat's alarm call the only sound. Then we rounded a bend in the dry torrent course we were following and came upon a withered elephant carcass, then another, then two more. Four elephants had been gunned down right alongside each other. Chris, a cool sardonic expression on his face, stepped back, the better to monitor the expression on mine.

'Welcome to the elephants' graveyard,' he said, 'and this is only the beginning. We know of at least twelve elephants and two rhino that have been shot in this immediate vicinity, most of them as they approached to drink at the spring, which is the only surface water in this area. After they kill an animal the poachers wait on top of a hill for at least a day, keeping a look-out and making sure no-one has heard or seen them. And now that the pressure is on them they're being a lot more careful about covering their tracks and getting rid of evidence. The latest strategy is to burn what's left of a carcass so that nothing remains. The ones we'll see today are old kills, and go back to the days before all the new precautions were necessary.'

We went on to the inert mass of a giraffe, intact except for a fillet sliced away from the backbone. 'Giraffe meat tends to be somewhat tough and grainy,' Chris said with heavy sarcasm, 'so these chaps only took the best cuts and left the rest. The bastards.'

All along the torrent course lay the forlorn collapsed shells of elephant carcasses with blank holes where their eyes had been, wiry eyelashes still in place; their scaly, tough soles had separated from the foot when the flesh had rotted away and now curled at the edges to resemble macabre saucepans. Soft downy *Stipagrostis* grass seeds, tumbled together by the wind, had collected into woolly balls and lodged in the carcasses' hollow corners. We found a python sunning itself beside a cavernous cadaver it had evidently claimed as its personal cave. On a hill-slope above one of the dead elephants, beneath a meagre tree, were the partially buried embers of a camp fire, the footprints

left by sandals cut from an auto tyre, the dismembered skeleton of a kudu bull, a cold drink bottle, and a rusted can.

We located the carcass Chris was after where it lay crumpled in a storm-water wash. 'She was probably mortally wounded and got this far before dying,' Chris briskly surmised. 'Obviously the poachers' lost track of her or the ivory wouldn't still be here.' The slender young tusks were in unusually good condition, unlike most ivory in western Namibia, which tends to be worn or broken at the tip owing to the elephants' digging in the rocky ground for roots and bulbs.

The tusks came away smoothly from their brittle bone sockets and, shouldering them, we returned to our vehicle. In driving back to Wêreldsend, where he was to spend the night, Chris opted to take a short cut on a track he thought he knew. But the route was deceptive, with forks and branches, and stretches where it merged into dry riverbeds. The sun set and the vague track blurred into a harsh emptiness of gravel haired over thinly by yellow stubble and scrub. Without Chris having said anything I suspected that we stood a good chance of getting lost.

Just then Lucas, riding in the open back, slapped urgently on the cab roof and yelled through the window, 'Turn left! turn left!'. Chris turned but grumbled, 'He's taking me back to the bloody fence-line. I want to go to the old cut-line and,' his voice increasing alarmingly in volume, 'he's taking me back to the bloody fence-line!'

A little later the track lost itself over rocky ground and it was too dark to see where to pick it up ahead. Without hesitation Chris gunned the engine and straight away we were careering over boulders, plunging onwards, although by now totally lost. Chris was muttering curses under his breath, yet it never seemed to cross his mind to slow down. To relieve his mounting tension, he suddenly bellowed, 'You're wrong, Lucas, you're bloody wrong. We should have taken the other road!'

Chris's agitation communicated itself to his dog, sitting between us, who in turn set up an impassioned howling. 'No, Fergie, no,' Chris roared. 'Shut up! I can't take that now.' Fergie flattened his ears nervously but, too caught up in the feverish commotion to contain himself, let loose another barrage of howls. In the cramped cab pandemonium reigned. I wondered if the situation was slipping out of control. We were still ploughing over tortuous ground and now Lucas started pounding on the roof again.

'Oh, Christ,' Chris said, braking unexpectedly. 'Sorry, Mitch. I can't hear a word that damn fool's saying.' They he jumped out to confer with Lucas. A moment later he got back in, jammed his pipe into his mouth and said in an entirely calm voice, 'Nearly there, Mitch, nearly there. Not far to go now.' And with Lucas guiding we soon picked up the track again. A bit later Chris said, 'Lucas was right; he's right, you know. He's got a fantastic memory. I've no mind for details. Sometimes I forget to fill in my daily notebook and when I'm backtracking I can say to Lucas, "Lucas, what did we do on the second?" and he'll say, "Oh, so and so," and he'll be absolutely right. They've got fantastic memories, but,' the proviso, added I suspected, as much because it was expected of him as anything else, 'they're also terrible bullshitters.'

The combating of poaching is the Damaraland Conservation Department's top priority and most serious concern. Within a week of our return from the ivory retrieval,

Left: *This severed head of a mountain zebra was the evidence that led to the arrest of the poachers*

an African living in Khorixas offered to sell mountain zebra meat to one of Chris's newly recruited game scouts, Nahor Howaseb, totally unaware that Nahor now worked for the game department. The flesh of the mountain zebra is a particular favourite of the Damaras and Hereros, being fine grained with white fat and sinews, unlike that of the plains zebra which is coarse, rank and dark red in colour with yellow fat and sinews.

After questioning the erstwhile meat wholesaler and learning where the zebra had been killed, Chris sent three scouts to investigate. On arrival at the spring where they had been told the poaching took place, and after a short search, they found a severed zebra's head wedged in the fork of a mopane tree. With this evidence they then proceeded to a nearby village where they accosted the two men whose names they had been given. At first, as is the custom, the men denied everything but then changed their story to say that yes, in fact two zebra had been caught, but completely accidentally in a gin-trap set quite legally to catch a marauding hyena. 'Let me see the gin-trap,' Nahor had retorted. 'If what you say is true there'll still be zebra hairs on the steel teeth,' whereupon the fabrications stopped and the poachers admitted that the two zebras had been taken in cable-snares specifically set for them.

In court the first man apprehended was found guilty on one count of illegally transporting game meat – 250 rand or three months – and on a second charge of selling game meat without a permit – a further 250 rand or three months, none of it suspended. The two hunters were each sentenced to a 1200 rand fine or twelve months for killing specially protected game, plus a sentence suspended for three years of 250 rand or three months for setting snares.

But Chris was doing his job too well, and had made enemies in Khorixas, the mean-spirited settlement he called home and one day, to strike at him, somebody poisoned his dog. 'The hardest thing,' he told me later, 'was old Fergie coming to me when he realised he was in bad trouble and there was nothing I could do – it was already too late.' His dog, his best friend really, died in his arms and Chris swore vengeance if he ever caught up with the person responsible.

Faced with the loss of his constant companion, Chris attempted a stoic public demeanour. 'I'll get another dog,' he said, 'a terrier, just like Fergie, call him Fergie II.' But he stared away into the distance as he spoke, and his voice lacked conviction. Fergie's personality, his intelligence, wackiness and loving nature were special, and Chris knew it.

# 5

# Fortress Mountains

To the south of Wêreldsend, below the Khorixas – Torra Bay road, lies an incandescent landscape of cones and pinnacles, sparse stone plains and desert buttes that decline southwards until it abruptly explodes into the jagged walls and violent rock-strewn mountains that palisade the Ugab River valley. These serrated biotic schist formations, of folded, marble-banded rock, then give way to the table top mountains of Damaraland in the Doras Crater area and along the Huab River, and further south looms the great granite mass of the Brandberg.

It is gaunt country and implacably hostile; I first saw it from the air, when I joined members of the Endangered Wildlife Trust in an aerial census of the region's larger mammals and birds. It is from this high-level perspective that the caustic scenic beauty of the place can most comfortably be appreciated. Newcomers are amazed by the land's toughness, and that anything can survive in it at all. I was there at the bitter end of a year-long drought that had severely exacerbated the wasteland prospect. Its appearance, its very nature, seemed so extreme – a burnt land of immensely wide views created from rock and sand, and forged in the igneous browns, greys, whites and muted pinks associated with pottery.

Our pilot, Peter Joffe, is also an EWT trustee. He flew the Centurion Cessna highwing in broad transects down rock corridors and across schist and gravel plains, while his passengers/observers called out information on the wildlife being seen – four springbok, one adult male, two adult females and a juvenile, sex undetermined; one lappet-faced vulture on nest; one rhino bull, which we were able to sex because of the rhino's habit of curling its tail over its back when it runs. The relayed data was duly fed into a tape recorder.

Aerial surveys are only one of the crucial conservation services provided by the Endangered Wildlife Trust, in the battle to save the northern Namib. The Johannesburg-based, privately funded organisation's involvement in Kaokoland and Damaraland started in 1978, after Clive Walker, its chairman at that time, visited the region together with Professor Fritz Eloff of Pretoria University. This initial fact-finding survey came about as a result of press reports which spoke of a poaching epidemic of staggering proportions. The reports had not been exaggerated, and the visitors were appalled by what confronted them there. Amongst other things they found more elephant and rhino carcasses than live animals, and became convinced that the situation was as desperate as they had been led to believe. They realised that, as a first step, it was critically important to alert the general public to what was going on behind the veil of bureaucratic secrecy drawn across the territory. It was becoming sickeningly apparent that more than mere official apathy was involved – certain government and military personnel not only sanctioned the actions but actively participated themselves.

In a hard-hitting article published in a 1978 issue of *African Wildlife* magazine, Clive Walker presented the depressing facts: 'Until 1977 Kaokoland was closed to all, bar government officials. No member of the public could go in without a permit and permits were rarely, if ever, given. Persistent rumours of poaching in the area came to a head in July 1977, when a press investigation revealed that officials in high places had been hunting elephant, as well as the rare black-faced impala. A former Commissioner General was one of those involved.

'During the controversy, a Windhoek reporter was sentenced to a jail term for refusing to disclose his sources of information (his conviction was set aside on appeal). Meanwhile a senior nature conservation official from the Department of Bantu Affairs, Henry Markram, claimed that he was transferred out of the territory after querying the shooting of an elephant. A Windhoek newspaper was about to publish the 16,000 word, "calm, cool, factual story of game dying" when the Defence Force froze further newspaper reports, and set up an inquiry into some of the allegations.' The findings of that inquiry were never to be made public.

As a practical first step to stop the killing, EWT, in conjunction with the South African Nature Foundation, and the Eugene Marais Chair of Wildlife Management of the University of Pretoria, funded Slang Viljoen's three year study into the status of the territory's larger mammals. Then, in the latter part of 1979, EWT conducted extensive aerial surveys which confirmed Slang's early reports that, far from improving, the conservation situation was rapidly deteriorating. In the light of the latest findings, the Endangered Wildlife Trust realised that further research into the biology of animals, that were being hunted into local extinction, was a hopeless endeavour. It was therefore decided to switch the emphasis towards law enforcement, and to that end the EWT combined resources with other non-government wildlife organisations from Namibia, South Africa, the United Kingdom and the United States to fund Garth Owen-Smith's anti-poaching field force, and at the same time to push for vigorous official efforts to stamp out the poaching.

The 100,000 rand spent since 1982 by these private bodies has paid handsome dividends, in that no elephant or rhino have been poached in Damaraland or Kaokoland since early 1983. However, negotiations, between the Department of Nature Conservation and the Damara authorities, to have a one million hectare desert park proclaimed, broke down in the beginning of 1984, leaving continued fears for the desert fauna's survival. In the same year the Namibia Wildlife Trust, two years after its inauguration, withdrew from the project for personal and financial reasons. A year

Right: *Gemsbok silhouetted against a setting sun that cauterises the parched land*

later, after a determined holding action, the EWT reluctantly gave up the struggle, and since then the US based SAVE Foundation has continued virtually singlehandedly to provide the salaries, vehicle and assistance needed for Garth, and his auxiliaries, to maintain anti-poaching and surveillance work. But there remains the unresolved question, as to whether the private sector can hold on, until such time as the responsible authorities come to some agreement, and establish meaningful control in the area.

This western enclave of central Damaraland we were flying over has experienced its share of desecration, and today is still supervised only sporadically by a few concerned individuals and rangers from the neighbouring Skeleton Coast Park. For many years, this remote corner has been subjected to continuous and widespread prospecting, that resulted in the giant open pit mine at Brandberg West, as well as a proliferation of small-scale mining operations. The apparent ruggedness of the country belies how sensitive it is to such scars. Moreover, prospecting activities have, through the years, opened up more and more tracks, while mining has led to the development of gravel roads, which have greatly facilitated the movement of motorized poachers through the area. In addition, the migration of game to and from the Skeleton Coast Park, in response to rainfall patterns, has been blocked by human habitation to the east, especially along the main river courses which the wildlife use as thoroughfares. Protected in the park, migratory gemsbok and springbok come under heavy hunting pressure when they move east, following rains in the pro-Namib.

I was anxious to see this hard primeval land from the ground, and happily accepted an invitation, extended by Blythe Loutit, to join her on one of her regular patrols into the area to collect botanical samples. After some radio confusion as to exactly when the trip was scheduled for, Blythe arrived at Wêreldsend one evening, a couple of weeks later, with her husband Rudi, who is warden of the Skeleton Coast Park, and Eccles, their chronically neurotic dog. They had driven up from Driftwood, their cottage on the Ugab River mouth at the southern entrance to the Skeleton Coast Park, where the three of them have lived in isolation for over six years. They regard themselves as extraordinarily lucky to be there.

The Skeleton Coast Park is widely believed to have been created, principally, as a device to prevent the Kaokoland and Damaraland homelands having access to the sea. Whatever the rationale behind its proclamation, park development has been limited to a single through road, the conversion of an abandoned mining camp into a tourist lodge and a seasonal campsite. The number of visitors was severely restricted, being limited almost exclusively to fishermen. Apparently, it had never occurred to the park's planners that anyone could value this stark, unencumbered coastline for its own sake, as the embodiment of nature at her most elemental.

Rudi, therefore, astonished his deskbound superiors when he proceeded to manage the park with a view to preserving its unblemished intrinsic wildness – vehicles were obliged to stay on the road, to prevent a myriad of unsightly prints that would remain impressed in the desert's crust for decades; the excavating of gravel pits to resurface the road was restricted and closely supervised; nor was litter and other forsaken items of human detritus left to disintegrate where they lay, as in the past. For those visitors who wished to do more than exploitatively catch unlimited quantities of fish, Rudi established overnight walking trails. He also encouraged his small team of rangers to pursue their own research projects, as a means to understanding the Skeleton Coast's ecological dynamics, while he himself used every moment prised from his heavy routine work-load to investigate a range of study subjects, from marine birds to porpoises.

Rudi has a dark sardonic countenance, and a faintly truculent air, that his crooked smile, spreading slow and dangerous as an oilslick, does nothing to offset. We had first met some years before, when I spent time on the Skeleton Coast, and on that occasion I can distinctly remember thinking that, behind Rudi's black impenetrable eyes, I detected a flared hint of madness. For those who have only made a casual acquaintance, it is the aura of psychosis Rudi radiates that leaves the most indelible impression. At first it is very disconcerting and of course he delights in provoking one's unease. Not content to leave it solely to others, he assiduously perpetuates and amplifies the tales that have grown up around his purported dementia. He also has a spontaneous and withering sense of humour, a rare gift in the almost uniformly austere desert community. Altogether, I found him to be a thoroughly accomplished and entertaining fellow.

He was at his best that evening when, after supper – fresh fish, thoughtfully provided by our guests – we settled down to coffee and talk. The conversation soon turned, as it inevitably does when discussing conservation, to the threat posed to the few remaining wildlife sanctuaries by explosively expanding human populations.

'The time's come to thin people out,' Rudi pronounced with finality.

'Easier said than done,' I replied, no doubt fatuously.

'It's bloody easily done,' Rudi frothed. 'Just give me the chance and I'll make Idi Amin look like Noddy.'

I suppose I should have been prepared for something of the sort – where he perceives people to be the cause of wildlife problems, Rudi's solutions are invariably homicidal. Later he railed against officialdom. 'The most corrupt, incompetent bunch of cretins God ever put breath into. Where do they go when they die?' He grinned evilly. 'Surely not the same place as us.'

During Rudi's derisive diatribes, his wife Blythe would turn to glance at him in mild astonishment every now and then, as if startled anew by his patented brand of off-the-wall iconoclasm. Eccles, the dog, stared up at his master with a catatonic fixity, perhaps trying to concentrate his mangled canine mind long enough to communicate some urgent inner message. From time to time the troubled hound would whine woefully, at which Rudi would break the beat of his leaping cogitation to snarl at him, then instantly took up the rhythm again. It was a virtuoso performance, and I could hardly stop laughing – insanity obviously has its charms – when towards midnight we trooped off to bed.

The next morning, Rudi continued his patrol northwards while Blythe and I set off for the south, towards the Springbok River. A warm east wind blew as Blythe drove her old shortwheel base Land Rover, with practised assurance, down a poor track that,

a year or two before, had been laboriously constructed by a local prospector's team of labourers. Our approach disturbed a party of suricates – a species of aridland mongoose – that streamed with flowing sinuous haste through the brittle yellow grass to the security of their burrow. We parked at a short distance to give them time to compose themselves, which they soon did, re-emerging cautiously at first, then with growing confidence. Before long they had assembled at the mouth of their burrow, sitting upright on their haunches to peer at us with a consuming curiosity, only breaking off to scan the sky for any sign of their mortal enemies, birds of prey. Satisfied that all was well, they energetically resumed foraging, digging for beetle larvae or overturning stones in search of scorpions and other small invertebrates.

Beyond the green slash, incised in brown basalt rubble, which demarcates the Springbok River, there are desert hills, and mountains burnt black by volcanic activity. We passed a field of strange, symmetrically rounded, black laval boulders that looked like a carefully arranged collection of cannonballs. To all points of the lonely horizon was a famished landscape of primordial rock and sand. Yet there was a lean and sinister splendour to this seemingly dead place. From the top of a stone ridge, enveloped by the great silence all around and the dry heat and hard light, I knew the quiet that comes with true awareness, with a sharpened exercising of the senses and with heightened consciousness. It is precisely that hardness to its edges, the uncertainty at its centre, that is desert Africa's allure. Confronted by a world utterly stripped of all adornments, sere and wind-whipped, where life seemed precarious and death so arbitrary, there came a more intense experience of my own being, and a great wild joy at being alive.

Further along, in the wall of a sandstone cliff, was a cave tunnelled out through the millennia by wind erosion. From its ceiling hung small brown bats, and darting rock martins came and went on the hot still air. We found a spring, cool and sweet, shaded from evaporation by the cave's overhang. On the gravel floor, amongst the scattered spoor of klipspringers and hyenas, there was the bold unmistakable print of a leopard. At the cave entrance, like palaeolithic god-heads, were great boulders of sandstone weathered into bizarre designs. Through the ages this wind-burnished cave, with its water and shade, must have provided a refuge for wild creatures and prehistoric man, and a shelter from which to ward off the great emptiness that pressed in from all sides.

Continuing south we reached one of the region's largest seasonal rivers, the Huab, at a point where a surface trickle of water debouches into a deep, reed-margined basin known as Peter's Pool. Our arrival sent a pair of red-knobbed coots spattering across the pool's surface, ending up in a swooshing belly-skate that carried them out of sight into the reedbed, from where they sounded a snorting alarm note. A duck that took off into the westering sun was scorched black and unidentifiable. I spotted what I was sure was a purple gallinule, just before it slipped from sight into the reeds.

The marvel of suddenly coming upon an oasis in the desert is beyond words. In celebration, washing and swimming, we remained at Peter's Pool for an hour, then went on south-eastward toward the Goantagab River.

The country we were travelling through is still represented on large scale maps by the names of the farms it was subdivided into, although the white farmers were bought

Left: *Remains of a rhino, poached when it came to drink from the only waterhole in the area*

out long ago, and the land incorporated into the Damara homeland. In the interim the farms have, for the most part, remained unoccupied, the prospects for settled ranching being too unpropitious. All that remain are the occasional crumbling abode homesteads, and the farm names which echo unfounded optimism – Probeer (Try), Goed Genoeg (Good Enough) – or one, Witwatersrand (White Water's Ridge), which perhaps evoked a nostalgia for a home left far behind, or maybe merely demonstrated a nice sense of irony.

Every so often we passed bleached zebra or antelope bones, left behind as a legacy of the recent drought. The key to survival for most desert-dwelling herbivores is nomadism, although relatively sedentary species, such as rhinos and giraffe, depend on low densities and/or utilization of exclusive pasture. In the Namib, the migratory species tend to remain in the dry, inhospitable western regions whenever conditions permit, probably because of the fewer predators there, and possibly innate wisdom dictates they do so, as a means of conserving emergency grazing in the east as a standing reserve. During the drought, fences prevented many migrating animals from following their traditional easterly movement, but some that got through entered Etosha via elephant-breaks in the game-proof fence and penetrated deep into the park, dramatically illustrating the distances they need to cover in the bad times if they are to have a chance of surviving.

Death by drought, as I experienced first-hand in western Etosha several years ago, is a grim business, ugly to the eyes and in the nostrils. There were too many carcasses to be readily processed by hyenas or other carnivores, and we were alerted to the presence of a recent casualty by the dry breeze, wafting a sickly sweet smell of putrefying flesh, a smell unusual in a place where a dead animal normally means food, and is quickly consumed. By the time rain fell, the tortured landscape was pocked with drought victims, now no more than hollow mounds of hard-baked skin, and sagging armatures of bone.

We had come to the Goantagab River, which here ran parallel to a mountain range of the same name. The dry watercourse, a tributary of the Ugab, was attractively set about with camel thorns and huge winter thorns. The mountain flank bristled with strange, swollen-stemmed moringas and fat, purple sterculias, with complementing commiphoras in shades of pink, white and rose. Off the track ahead, two kudu cows and a young male cantered back into the riparian scrub before stopping in a screen of thin grey saplings to inspect us, as if aware that the thin, silver stripes on their coats merged perfectly with the vegetation. A swallow-tailed bee-eater, hawking an insect on the wing, spun iridescent shafts of blue light in the waning afternoon sun.

The day was late and, as we were not far from the Doros Crater, which Blythe wanted to visit the following day, we stopped to set up camp and collect firewood before night closed in. Pacing along the sandy riverbed in search of dead acacia logs, I marvelled once again how, in contrast to the colour-dissipating glare of the long day, the colours in the soft last light were so pure, so vivid, that they acquired a brief energy of their own, and scintillated. In the far distance, the haunted Brandberg – a great shard of rock thrust upward from the earth, its summit the highest point in Namibia – floated pink in the southern sky, like a pale heavenly fire.

Soon aftet sunset, barking geckoes commenced their urgent staccato chattering, and far away a jackal wailed. Chased by a light breeze, the flames of our campfire scittered, rising and falling. Over the fire, while we waited for supper to grill, Blythe talked about her life in the desert, how she came to be there and her hopes for the future.

Her family came from Pietermaritzburg, the sleepy provincial capital of Natal, and after leaving school, Blythe stayed on in town to work, first for the Natal Parks Board and later, in 1969, as a technical artist at the Natal Museum. During that time she developed her artistic skills doing freelance botanical illustrations, including a booklet called *Composites of Natal*. She then went on to work for the Botanical Research Institute in Durban, as a technician and artist. But, her imagination fired by tales of Angola's unspoilt spaces, she set off for the remote West African territory, and immediately fell in love with it. Its complementary blend of southern European and African she found to be irresistible, but by the time she arrived, the war for independence was already well advanced.With great regret, Blythe recognised that there was no immediate future for her in that troubled paradise, which before long was to degenerate into anarchy.

She returned to South Africa, and there followed several restless years, when she worked for various conservation organisations until, by now married to Rudi, she once again headed north, this time to Namibia. Rudi joined the Conservation Department and eventually, in 1978, they were posted to the Skeleton Coast. Blythe had been altogether unprepared for the spell the Namib would cast over her. She discovered in the desert silences and vistas the validity of all her artistic impulses, impulses which locate their spirit in the elemental, in nature, in the life of wild animals and primitive people, and in instinct and passion.

Working in oils and watercolours, Blythe's art flourished and received increasingly wide acclaim. She was commissioned to do the illustrations for *Trees and Shrubs of Etosha* and *Grasses of Namibia* as well as the plant studies in the book by Clive Walker and Don Richards, *Walk Through the Wilderness*. There also followed a successful series of gallery exhibitions, of which, Blythe recalled with quiet pleasure; 'The Etosha collection was the most exciting; the work was very spontaneous and fresh, and the show a complete sell-out.'

Blythe's field studies along the course of the Ugab River started out as a plant survey that concentrated on the various commiphora species, while at the same time drawing up a general checklist for the area. On her first outing – which, like nearly all the others that were to follow, meant going alone, except for her dog, into the desert for days on end – she noticed soup plate-sized footprints leading up to a commiphora she was interested in. With great excitement she recognised them as those of a rhino and rushed home to tell Rudi of her discovery. On her next visit she sighted a rhino cow with a calf, a pair that subsequently became central to Blythe's study and which she named 'Ulundi' and 'Nqabas', the latter being the African name for rhino.

From the moment Blythe realised that she shared her desert Eden with so unlikely a denizen as *Diceros bicornis*, she was totally absorbed by the fact and its implications. She determined to spend five consecutive days, over the full moon period, in the field each month in order to track rhino movements and browse preference – work which would involve a great deal of following-up on foot.

The beginning of Blythe's project coincided with the extremely impoverished conditions that existed at the tail end of the drought, which made her findings all the more interesting. Despite having to walk long distances in search of food, the eight rhinos – six identified and two known only by their tracks – in her study area did not lose condition, probably, Blythe speculates, due to their low densities.

After two years of observations and records, Blythe decided to ask for professional help, and approached Professor Gideon Louw of Cape Town University's Zoology Department, who came to visit the Ugab and advised her how best to make a meaningful research contribution. As a result, once all of Blythe's data concerning the rhinos' daily activity patterns, seasonal movements, feeding preferences, drinking intervals and social communication is collated, a fascinating picture will emerge regarding the desert rhino's ecology and their ability to make a living in such a hostile environment. This, in turn, will help determine the number of rhinos the Ugab environs can support, and whether the present low population can be supplemented by translocating desert rhinos from farming districts, where the threat of poaching is a constant reality.

Early the next morning, after a dawn mug of coffee, we drove slowly down the Goantagab's sandy course until we came upon fresh rhino spoor. Blythe recognised the track by its skew back heel as that of an adult bull she has named TM, after the initials of a friend who was with her when she first saw the rhino. To standardise her observations, Blythe follows a spoor for exactly an hour, recording the plants that have been browsed. We thus set out on foot to comply with her regular procedures, noting how the bull had slowly browsed along a well-used route that would eventually bring it to water, and Blythe patiently tallied the number of bites taken from a variety of bushes and creepers the rhino had sampled.

Blythe has found that the southern desert rhinos use eighty per cent of the plants available to them. One of her most interesting discoveries came in the Ugab River, where occur intermittent 'gorras' (wells dug in the bed by wild animals) and short stretches of open water, which have a strange habit of 'rising' between August and November – usually the driest time of the year. This rising causes a regeneration of vegetation in the riverbed but, in spite of the bed's lushness, rhinos do not spend much time feeding there. Well-worn paths show that they move into extremely harsh rocky gullies where vegetation is very sparse. The paths respond to the topography in a remarkable way, winding through krantzes and gaps, always by the easiest route. Yet the rhinos nevertheless expend a great deal of energy, particularly during the dry season, negotiating trails that often go up to high rocky outcrops. As it has been shown that rhinos seek out certain plants at certain times of the year, Blythe has speculated that mountain slope vegetation is favoured during dry months because it is succulent – both more nutritious and retaining more water. In the case of the *Euphorbia virosa*, an unlikely looking specimen of preferred forage, rhinos will climb a perilous path up and obliquely across great slabs of loose shale-like schist, to get to the plant, which usually

Right: *Flowering* Euphorbia virosa

grows in inaccessible places. Once they reach it, they use their prehensile top lip to peel the spikes off like a banana skin, then eat from the core. With commiphoras, they push their heads into the shrub and break off the branches with their horns to get at the succulent stem.

When Blythe follows the rhinos themselves, rather than merely their tracks, she first registers the ambient temperature and, using a hand-held anemometer, takes the wind direction and speed, all factors that influence a rhino's browsing activity. She has found that browsing usually takes place in the early daylight hours, in late afternoon and during the night. In the winter months, when the herbage is of low nutritional value, the rhinos resort to bulk feeding; if there is a cool wind blowing, they may continue browsing throughout the day. In the wake of good rains, with nutritious forage freely available, their volume intake is reduced. Blythe also collects specimens of rhino droppings to be sent off for analysis, to determine the mineral content and digestibility of the plants they have eaten.

In all the time she has spent in close contact with rhinos, Blythe has only once had a serious incident, but that very nearly ended in tragedy. She had been tailing her favourite study subjects, Ulundi and Nqabas, downwind for most of one morning, during the course of which the cow had dimly and uneasily become aware of a presence at the edge of her perceptions. Then Blythe had stumbled and dropped her notebook; its pages fluttering in the breeze had been enough to trigger Ulundi's taut temper. Instantly, with her juvenile calf in close attendance, she charged towards the source of the disturbance.

Blythe hurriedly backed away, shouting in the hope of scaring the rhinos off, but they came on without faltering. In her agitation, Blythe half-dropped, half-threw her camera, then her binoculars at the looming, ferocious cow and, when all else failed, turned to make a last desperate run for it, tripped over a bounder and went down. The fall very likely saved her life. Wedged between rocks, with the rhinos towering over her, she reacted instinctively by lashing out with her foot, and connected Ulundi on the lip with the sole of her boot. That sudden physical contact and Blythe's shouts of 'Go away! Go away!' broke the rhino's nerve, and she turned and led her calf away at a very fast trot. Blythe came shakily to her feet to watch them thundering off, and only when they had almost disappeared from sight did she realise that she was still yelling 'Go away!' at the top of her voice.

It had been a very close thing, and Blythe had had a bad scare. She had been alone, as usual, and if she had been gored and unable to reach the radio in her vehicle, she would, in all likelihood, not have been missed until too late. But a week later she was back in the field again, only this time armed with a new resolution to be more careful in the future.

At the end of the hour, we returned to the Land Rover we had left parked in the shade of a broad-canopied camel thorn. We had it in mind to brew up a pot of tea, but were hurried on our way by a visitation of irksome pests. First to arrive were a cloud of persistent mopane bees, although the distribution of the mopane tree, with which they are usually associated, reaches its southernmost limit a few kilometres north of the

Goantagab. Next, we became aware that the shaded loose sand beneath the camel thorn was infested with tampans, a species of 'soft tick' that is related to, but very different in biology from the 'hard tick', commonly found on domestic animals. These miniature monsters live in large colonies which burrow up to twenty centimetres below the sand surface. They are disturbed by shifts in the sand, caused by any large animal moving around in their vicinity, whereupon they swarm to the surface and attempt to locate the animal by means of carbon dioxide receptors, which detect molecules exhaled in the breath, or emanated from the skin.

Once the tampans have located and attached to an animal, they will, within ten to twenty minutes, feed to repletion on its blood, detach, and burrow superficially into the sand again. While feeding, a neurotoxin is secreted by the tampan's salivary gland; should a whole colony attack an animal, the toxin has a paralysing effect, ensuring a stationary source of food, and sometimes resulting in the death of young or weak animals. Altogether a good enough reason for us to move on without delay.

We departed the river at a point where dusky sunbirds – the males, in contrast to most other sunbird species, almost as drab as the females – dipped long curved bills to extract the nectar of winter flowers. Our track wound down into the Doros Crater, where a family group of springbok bounced across the flats with rubber-sprung legs and arched backs.

At a granite outcrop we examined a series of smooth, water-eroded rock basins that act as a rain catchment. Blythe knew of four rhinos that regularly drank there, and their spoor was everywhere. In the past, one of the rhinos had used its horn to break down the stout branches of a sterculia, no doubt to chew the wood fibre for moisture after the pools had dried out. A solitary boulder had attained a high polish, after decades of use as a rhino rubbing post. Bulbuls and laughing doves fell silent, waiting for us to go, and strange dull-brown darting creatures called dassie rats scuttled out of sight into rock crevices. We were probably the only people to have passed that way in a week, and we were an intrusion.

In the thickening midday heat, the rough track unfurled northwards until we entered the Twyfelfontein Valley, its flat floor covered with grass and aromatic herbs and enclosed by tall circling cliffs. The reddish sandstone krantzes and boulders seemed almost to glow in the heat, but beneath the fallen rock slabs, overhangs, arches and shallow caves, were pools of deep shade. There is also the perennial spring from which the valley takes the name Twyfelfontein or Doubtful Spring, given it by a farmer of little faith. Shelter and water, and the wild animals that once roamed there, were valuable assets to a hunting people – that Stone Age men had lived here is attested to by the more than 2000 engravings that they laboriously hammered, chiselled, gouged, pecked and scratched into the sandstone slabs. It is the greatest collection of rock engravings in Africa, although very little research has been done on them.

The subject matter of these engravings comprises roughly three sections – the animals hunted, their spoor, and strange abstract or geometrical forms. Most appear in monochromatic silhouette, with red or maroon the predominant colour. Unlike elsewhere in southern Africa, where rock paintings and engravings are nearly always in

different localities to each other, at Twyfelfontein they are both represented. In contrast to the engravings, people are a dominant motif of the paintings, whereas animal hoofprints and abstract geometrical designs are conspicuous by their absence.

Until recently it was impossible to carbon-date the engravings, but finally a breakthrough was made. In the past they were estimated to date back 1000 years; now the evidence points to their being far older – at least 8000 years – and the sound of flaked quartz chipping against sandstone may have been heard here as long ago as 10,000 years. Yet, although the artwork provides a fascinating window to a past culture and civilization, it is uncertain exactly who the artists were. The Bantu-speaking Negroids have no tradition of rock painting or engraving, and there is little evidence to suggest that the Damaras contributed anything more than later and somewhat crude works. This leaves the Bushmen, and at this stage the best that can be stated is that either the ancestors of the present-day San, or perhaps an extinct Bushmanoid race, created most of the rock art. Equally uncertain is the genesis of the art itself. Whether it developed locally or accompanied immigrant groups remains unclear. Were painters and engravers mutually exclusive? Were different peoples responsible for the two art forms? Whatever the truth, in the Twyfelfontein Valley the rock art is the only sign left of its occupation by the Old People, who long ago went into hiding in the earth.

Left: *In the Twyfelfontein Valley are more than two thousand rock engravings left by a vanished tribe*

CHAPTER

# 6

# Down The Hoanib

Sesfontein was the jumping-off point on a journey I made, in the company of Garth
Owen-Smith and Elias Hambo, down the course of the dry Hoanib River
westwards through the Namib Desert and on to the Skeleton Coast.

The Hoanib River rises on farmlands west of the township of Kamanjab, traverses
what was once part of the Etosha Game Reserve and from near the Kamdescha
veterinary gate to its mouth, forms the boundary dividing Kaokoland from
Damaraland. West of Khowarib Gorge, the broad acacia-studded Hoanib River valley
is enclosed by rugged dolomite ranges, at the base of which languishes the secluded
settlement of Sesfontein. Not long ago Sesfontein was still a secret place, a world unto
itself, but like so much else in modern Africa it has been opened up and badly used – its
despoilation is almost complete.

Sesfontein – Six Fountains – takes its name from a series of artesian springs from
which millions of litres of water well up every day. Occupation by man's ancestors of
the Sesfontein oasis, at the edge of a westering thirst-land, has probably been
continuous or nearly so since hominid creatures first appeared on the scene. The first
known inhabitants were the hunter-gathering Damaras and San Bushmen, who were
dispossessed during the course of the sixteenth century by the Bantu-speaking, cattle-
herding Hereros, pushing southwards from Angola. The relationship, where any
existed, between the fierce pastoralists and the small hunters was that of master and
servant. This state of affairs ended around 1850 with the invasion from the south of
marauding bands of Nama Hottentots. The first of these intruders were the Topnaars,
who had for centuries lived in the dunes of Walvis Bay and at the mouth of the Kuiseb
River. They linked up later with the formidable Swartboois, one of the oldest Nama
clans and an offshoot of the parent Red Nation. Through their contacts with
missionaries and traders, the Swartboois had acquired some of the accoutrements of
civilization, including the Bible and the gun.

The Namas established their base at Sesfontein, and from there they raided the
Herero herds with remorseless thoroughness. The nomadic Hereros, living in widely-
spaced family groups were unable, at short notice, to organise effective resistance to the
Nama's swift-striking horseback commandos. The loss of all their cattle caused a social
and moral crisis of great proportions among the Herero. Their impoverishment was

more than an economic disaster – the inferior hunter-gatherer way of life they were forced to lead as a consequence undermined the tribe's cultural self-assurance and stability on the widest possible scale. They were branded as 'Tjimba' – the aardvarks – because their destitution had reduced them to digging in the ground for food. The hegemony of the Hereros had been displaced devastatingly by the irresistible combination of the horse and the gun; the predatory Namas had become the dominant people at Sesfontein.

But events were moving fast. In 1884 the German flag was hoisted over 'Luderitz-land' on Namibia's southern coastline, and in the following year agreements were signed with various tribes, culminating in a formal declaration of German protectorate over the whole territory excluding the British enclave at Walvis Bay. It wasn't long before the Damara chief, Cornelius Goreseb, recognised that 'the tribes have had their day; the white man is now in control of Damaraland'.

In the remote Sesfontein Valley, however, the status quo lingered on. The Namas – in particular the combative, more numerous Swartboois – continued in their plundering ways. Having ransacked the whole of Kaokoland, they crossed the Kunene into Angola and enriched themselves at the expense of the helpless tribes living there. Then, in 1897, a calamity intervened that deprived the Swartboois of their spoils at the same time as it devastated the rest of the country. An epidemic of rinderpest – a viral cattle plague from Asia that had raged like a tempest down the entire length of Africa – swept across the South African frontier and into Namibia. So virulent was the scourge that it has been estimated that 95 percent of the tribal herds were struck down – a catastrophe that was quickly followed by the spectre of famine.

To add to their great misfortunes of that year, the Swartboois rose up against German rule in a rebellion that had been provoked by succession rivalries. Their action proved a fatal mistake. The Herero chiefs Manasse and Samuel Maherero, and the southern Nama leader Hendrik Witbooi, honouring their treaties with the Germans, collaborated with the *Schutztruppe*, to crush the revolt. In a campaign lasting four months, the Swartboois sustained grievous casualties from which the demoralised tribe was never able to recover. Their lands were confiscated and in 1906 the survivors were settled on the Sesfontein reserve with the remnants of the Topnaars. War and malaria and a terrible world-weariness debilitated the Nama and leached their vitality, while breeding with other tribes had diluted their ethnicity; the time may be at hand when the last pure-blooded Khoikhoi, the hard-tongued 'men of men', will vanish into the earth.

To a remarkable degree, Sesfontein is a microcosm of the fortunes and fates of Namibia's peoples. On the village's periphery there are the ruins of an old German fort – a crumbling epitaph to a failed colonial dream. The fort was built in 1902, in the wake of the war with the Swartboois, as the north-western line of defence in the Reichstag's burgeoning imperial ambitions. Its architect was Captain Victor Franke whose duty it was, thirteen years later during World War I, to surrender the German forces to the invading South African army. In a turbulent thirty years the German era had come and gone. Now, seventy years on, it is the South Africans who are preparing to leave. Their going follows a seemingly immutable pattern, a dynamic cycle of change, of rise and fall

and occasional resurgence, that has prevailed in this troubled land where, as in the Afro-Asian symbolism of the snake of eternity swallowing its tail, all is in flux, all comes full circle, with no beginning and no end.

On the morning of our departure from Wêreldsend, a cloying sea mist – brought about by a relatively cold high-pressure system that had developed on the previous afternoon – penetrated far into the hinterland and shrouded the camp. The haunted desert air was very strange and still; all about seethed a murky, intangible world, monochromatic and foreshortened, as in an under-sea tableau. Condensation filmed the narrow slender leaves of the wild ebonies, dripping slow drops from their tips. We drove out through a grey mist curtain beyond which little was revealed.

The fog evaporated as we proceeded north, and we arrived at the cluster of sapling-and-daub huts at Warmquelle in a bright burst of sunshine. As on the occasion when we had come by to report the giraffe-poaching incident, the village's headman, Joshua Kangombe, was firmly in place beneath a spreading ringwood tree. As before, he sat on a frayed folding stool, doodling in the dust with his silver-tipped walking stick. 'Doesn't he ever move?' I asked. 'Sometimes,' replied Garth. 'Then he's OUT, now he's IN. He's the headman and that's his executive suite.'

'But he never seems to do anything,' I said.

'He's shuffling paper, so to speak – passing the time of day until something important comes along.'

We stopped to be sociable and because Garth had been asked to explain the territory's hunting and conservation regulations to an assembly of elders. The men gathered together to exchange formal greetings with their white visitors, calling 'Moro, moro' (good morning) and offering handshakes all round. Chairs were brought for Garth and me – Elias had taken himself off to visit what passes for a shop in Warmquelle – and we settled in the shade. Pipe-smokers hawked and spat into the dust; I noticed a steel-jawed gin-trap off to one side, an ugly piece of machinery but very effective against lions and hyenas.

An interpreter, in a red cowboy shirt and dove-grey slacks, translated Garth's words into Herero as he first introduced me and then went on to the subject of the meeting. 'I've come here today because Joshua has asked me to speak to you about the problems of the game. There have been people that have had stiff sentences and there have been some hard feelings concerning that.' A man wearing blue overalls and a rolled-up balaclava said, 'Explain to us the law and we can talk about it.'

Against a subdued background cacophony of children playing, cocks crowing and the chidings of hornbills competing with fowls for scraps, Garth continued: 'I first came here in 1970 and met Joshua and some of the other elders here today. Then, on the other side of that mountain, there was a game reserve. At that time I was told by the people that all they wanted was grass – they would not harm the game. We saw they needed grazing and gave them permission to use the park, and the wild animals were left undisturbed. Then I went away; now that I'm back I see that all the game is gone. The drought was bad, I know that. I'm here now to try and save the little that remains. But I find myself in a difficult position. I've known Joshua for many years but now it's my job to stop his people hunting. Some have gone to court and received stiff

Above: *A Herero woman in traditional dress carries a pumpkin from the village garden*

Below: *Old woman in the Damaraland quarter of Sesfontein*

sentences, which is a hard thing in these hard times. I'm here to find out how to stop the poaching and still see to it that the people's interests are understood and respected.'

Further talk was temporarily interrupted by the grating, hoarse complaints of a hobbled donkey. One old gentleman stood up from the upturned tin drum he was using as a seat, walked off a few paces, urinated and then returned to the circle. A hen leading a cheeping column of chicks scratched at the compacted soil; the donkey's tirade wound down with a high-pitched volley of pitiful hiccups. Garth went on: 'Some animals, such as elephants and rhinos, are not hunted for meat but for profit. They are state game and may not be hunted without a permit from Windhoek. If there are problems with elephants raiding gardens, the villagers must contact a ranger who will try and drive them away, but if that doesn't work he will shoot them. You may chase them away but not kill them. Any man that owns stock has the right to protect it and to kill a marauding lion, leopard, cheetah or hyena. But if they live apart from man they must not be molested. All the law requires is that, if a "problem" predator is killed, it must be reported to Chris Eyre in Khorixas. Then, if a permit is obtained, the pelt may be sold. Ordinary game – kudu, springbok, gemsbok and so on – may be hunted in the hunting season but first a permit must be granted. Each year the local government decides how many of each species may be hunted. But this year, as happened last year, the hunting season will stay closed because there are so few animals left.'

A grizzled patriarch, wearing a tea cosy for a hat and with a lens missing from his spectacles, emphasising a staring blind eye, introduced himself as a minor headman and said: 'It is true that most of the game is wiped out. We have seen it happen in the last few years. It is good now that it is to be protected. Perhaps *muhona* could also speak to my people stationed at the posts away from Warmquelle.'

A general discussion followed, each man speaking his piece to the end without interruption. Everyone had been polite and in agreement that something must be done to conserve the game. I had no doubt that if it were left up to the elders something would be done, but I also had a nagging unease that theirs was an outdated wisdom. Despite the fact that to this day Herero society remains on the whole deeply conservative and resistant to new ideas, it cannot stay entrenched for much longer. The rule of the chiefs will collapse along with the whole tribal system. As it is, the chiefs have become targets for revolutionary assassins who accuse them of co-operating with the white authorities; and as protection they have been assigned a well-armed 'home-guard', whose salaries are paid by the government.

Although anxious to see social political reform come to Namibia, Garth wanted it filtered through the old guard of traditionalist headmen. When I pointed out that change was most likely to come by way of the 'young Turks', his 'dark glasses brigade' of acculturated Africans, he recognised the truth of the observation without liking it or me for having made it. Thereafter, to register his disapproval, he insisted on referring to them as 'your friends, the young radicals'. That they were no friends of mine, nor I of theirs, was beside the point. It was sufficient to lump us together as enemies of the old order. Even though I certainly am not its enemy, I simply do not think the old order stands a chance.

At least in the rural areas, though, the tribal structure remains shakily in place and by working through it Garth has been satisfyingly successful in spreading his message. The meeting had gone off well. It closed just as a big tabby cat, with strains of wild cat in its pelage and oddly folded-forward ears, entered the circle, sneezed three times and left again. The cat's quirky entreé was bizarrely on cue, or so it seemed to me; I took it as a sign that while man presumes to determine her course, it is nature who will have the last apocalyptic word.

We ate lunch – salami and pickles on black pumpernickel – at the nearby Ongongo artesian spring, where a small waterfall forms a transculent, sweet-water pool; a veiled retreat set about by tall trees and adorned with ferns dyed bright viridian. The pale swollen roots of a Namaqua fig (*Ficus cordata*) clove to the smooth rock-face.

It was shaded and cool in the grotto; the water, when I dived in, was bracingly chill. My plunge frightened a water snake, which hastened out of harm's way with a rapid sidewinding motion. Thirsty blue-black wasps came and went on the listless breeze, droning close to my head without threat or alarm. The water was so cold that I soon got out and lay flat on a boulder to let the sun dry me, beguiled by the sensuous sound of running water in a desert. A forlorn laughing dove contributed its own descending liquid notes.

On the flatlands adjoining the spring, Carl Schlettwein, a prominent farmer during the German period in the early years of this century, had turned the soil in an attempt to raise experimental crops of maize, wheat, barley and tobacco. Schlettwein had epitomised the colonist's frontier spirit and enterprise, as well as the courage of those intrepid souls who were often first to penetrate unsettled regions so far beyond the limit of European civilization. Equally typical were his narrow sensibilities where the indigenous Africans were concerned. He maintained that the Germans were 'the lords of the land', and that 'our policies will be those of masters. We shall make people realise that we Germans are the masters of the country and the natives the servants, whose welfare depends on the advantage of their masters ... Government measures must provide for a situation in which the native realises that it is in his best interests to take up work.'

Yet there is a trace of ambivalence in Schlettwein's attitudes, mirrored by many of his fellow settlers, wherein he professes an appreciative respect for individual Africans and concedes there were some 'to whom one take's off one's hat' – but this does little to ameliorate the imbedded contempt implicit in his self-serving philosophy. It was the first governor of *Deutsche Südwestafrika*, the high-minded classicist and professional soldier Major Theodor Leutwein, who – with a candour that was out of step with the prevailing sentiments – recognised the situation for what it was: 'The colour of a man's skin is supposed to determine his worth, so that in the colonies every white man is regarded as a "superior being" ... The Europeans flooding into Hereroland were inclined, with their inborn feeling of belonging to a superior race, to appear as members of a conquering army, even though we had conquered nothing.'

Today, little enough rer ins of Schlettwein's endeavours at Warmquelle. The soil has been impoverished through constant use and requires infusions of fertilizer, which has only tardily been attended to. The year I was there, a chemical deficiency – probably nitrogen – had brought on yellow streaks in the leaves of the mielie crop and the plants

had failed to produce cobs. In the dusty, drooping fields I gazed upon the broken bones of Schlettwein's homestead and irrigation schemes. The land and air were redolent of hope, frustration and overwhelming defeat. The striving, the pain of that lonely bigoted man; and to what purpose? All seemed pointless, as if all the waste and loss in life, the harm one brings to oneself and others were part of a cruel cosmic joke.

In the wake of the drought that had decimated their livestock, the disastrous crop failure brought the hard-scrabble Herero villagers at Warmquelle face to face with chronic deprivation – small wonder they turned to the scanty wildlife as a last resort. When a tribesman becomes seriously hungry and his children are malnourished, when his fields cannot produce a harvest nor his pastures sustain his stock, how can he respond to the nebulous concept of game conservation? It is becoming increasingly apparent that if anything is to be saved, naturalists can no longer afford to avoid concern in human affairs. Whether imbued with humanitarian ideals or not, it is only by solving the human problems that they can conserve the things they love.

Wild animals, like many people in Africa, face an unstable and turbulent future. As the human population in Africa is likely to double within the next twenty years, the conflict and competition between man and wildlife must inevitably increase. In the last fifty millennia, man has caused the extinction of many species and local populations, including populations of man himself; but he risks destroying more species in the next few decades than in all his previous history. Yet ultimately we are the endangered species. *Homo sapiens* is perceived to stand at the top of the pyramid of life; but the pinnacle is a precarious station and there are considerable omens that the plundered earth's retribution will be accomplished by those who despoiled it.

The short road from Warmquelle to Sesfontein winds westwards through undulating park-like valleys embellished with stately camel thorns and the emblematic tree of Africa, the umbrella thorn. It was very pleasant country, though, un-encumbered and quintessentially African. Africans plied the road in donkey carts, on bicycles and on foot, keeping to their own time. A lone ground squirrel, fogged by our dust, stood bolt upright on its hindlegs to watch man pass. Birds swarmed – hornbills, babblers, rollers and a pygmy falcon that got up ahead of us with a limp lizard clutched in its talons.

The prospect moved Elias, sitting between Garth and me, to sudden vehemence. 'You have heard the saying, "Where Herero cattle graze, that is Hereroland"?' he burst out. 'Well, that saying is the truth. It is also true that the Damaras always lived in this country but in the mountains, not on the plains where the Hereros had their herds. The Damaras are not real people. Well, they are people of course but not proper people, they are more like baboons. It was the whites that made them into real people and gave them land. But now they want to be rid of the whites, so what good did it do the whites to be kind to the Damaras?' Then he lapsed into a brooding silence.

Elias's unabashedly racist diatribe was in the style current throughout black Africa, a point of view once thought to be the exclusive preserve of the whites. Elias likes it to be known that he is a Herero and is an ardent champion of Herero rights, particularly where he perceives a conflict of interests with the Damaras. His attitude seemed extraordinary, considering that he not only lived in Damaraland, more or less on the

Left: *Distress and despair at drought relief camp – Porus, west Kaokoland*

sufference of the Damara authorities, but had a *de facto* wife who was Damara. I suspected that his fulminations against the Damaras were reserved for his white audiences and it occurred to me that, at heart, he was more of a snob than anything else. Only later did I hear, in a roundabout way, that he was in fact half Damara himself – which accounted for his very dark skin and short, thickset build – and that his Damara father had worked as a cattleherd for a wealthy Herero *muhona*. One can only wonder at the effect the stigma of his father's tribal and social inferiority, and the discrimination that must have accompanied it, had on the young boy who went on to become a proud man with a very heavy chip on his shoulder. At the very least it resulted in a total rejection of his paternal origins, and his bitterness could only have been compounded by the realisation that he would never be accepted in his own right by the intensely class-conscious Herero aristocracy.

Elias's complaints regarding the Damaras invariably revolved around the question of land ownership, an issue that is at the heart of practically all Namibia's past and present disputes. In spite of the vastness of the country and the paucity of people, the competition for fertile pastures has provoked internecine quarrels and genocidal wars.

The cycle of incessant tribal feuds – waged with the aim of annihilating the opposition whilst appropriating their livestock and grazing lands – began more than a decade before the first traders and missionaries arrived, and fifty years before Germany declared its protectorate. Into this whirling flux came the military might and technocracy of the Germans, the latest and most formidable of the combatants. The new colonists, employing treaties or force as the situation demanded, established themselves in the country, and their confrontation with the Africans frequently culminated in uprisings in the areas of major settlement.

By 1903 about one quarter of what had been Hereroland had been sold to the Germans, much of it by the dissolute paramount chief Samuel Maherero. His right to do so was angrily challenged by Herero headmen, who pointed out that traditionally land was communally owned by the whole tribe. But Samuel had relied on the force of German arms to guarantee his paramountcy; he had entered into a long-standing pact with the German government and had, to all intents and purposes, become beholden to them. The Germans thought they knew their man. 'He claimed only his rights,' Governor Leutwein noted disdainfully. 'His duties were sacrificed to his search for pleasure.'

Yet Samuel Maherero recognised the expanding German presence both as a source of support in his conflicts with other Herero chiefs and as a threat to his own people. There was in fact alarm among the various African tribes that German encroachment upon their lands would never stop – a process that would before long undermine their sovereign rights and ultimately their whole way of life. Moreover, white rule had reached a point where every European exercised private police jurisdiction over the tribesmen, meting out corporal punishment and occasionally killing those they regarded as transgressors. In the few instances where such offences were brought to court, the settlers were either acquitted or given absurdly lenient sentences. Nothing damaged the trust between the races more than this scandalous inequality before the law. 'Racial hatred had become rooted in the very framework of justice,' remarked the exasperated Leutwein. Irrevocably the Hereros came to realise that German rule meant not only the loss of their lands and subsequent economic ruin, but personal humiliation as well.

In the end, Samuel Maherero's tribal links proved stronger than all others; although he is said not to have taken the initiative, he committed himself to a general war and successfully unified the Herero in a tidal wave of revolt. On 12 January 1904, he gave the order that all German men, except missionaries, should be killed. The attack was a complete surprise and more than a hundred farmers and soldiers were cut down. So impenetrable was the secrecy surrounding the planning of the uprising that at the time it erupted Leutwein and most of his troops were six hundred kilometres to the south, quelling a rising by the Bondelswart Namas.

In the early stages of the war the Hereros seized the advantage, but at no time had Samuel Maherero ever entertained any illusions as to the enormity of the risks involved. In a letter to the son of Chief Zacharias at Otjimbingwe, he wrote: 'Your father knows that if we rebel we will be annihilated in battle since our people are practically unarmed and without ammunition, but the cruelty and injustice of the Germans have driven us to despair, and our leaders and our people both feel that death has lost its terrors because of the conditions under which we now live.'

During the months of February and March 1904, 1576 officers and men, 10 pieces of artillery, 6 machine guns and 1000 horses arrived to reinforce the German troops. Leutwein was now able to put 2500 men into the field to confront 10,000 Hereros. Artillery, machine guns and rapid-fire rifles gave the Germans overwhelming superiority in firepower but it also tied them to a bulky, slow-moving and highly vulnerable supply train, without which their weapons were useless. Conversely, the Hereros made skilful use of their knowledge of the terrain to pursue guerilla tactics effectively. The German troops were inexperienced in bush warfare and the reinforcements were thoroughly daunted by the country's harshness. 'Everything looked so dead, so bleak, so deserted,' an officer wrote in dismay on first sighting the coastline. 'There were no palms, no woods, no trees, no shrubs: only stones, rocks and sand ... We gazed at the shore with anxiety and astonishment.' In Hereroland the technology of the West encountered the stark elemental forces of nature, and Western technology initially proved to be deficient.

In the early months of the war both sides sustained heavy losses. The Berlin government blamed Leutwein – whom they had forbidden to negotiate for peace – for the lack of military success. The general staff decided to replace him with General von Trotha, a seasoned colonial fighter with a well-earned reputation for ferocity. A decade earlier, in German East Africa (Tanzania), he had ruthlessly suppressed the Hehe, who had been fighting against the appropriation of their lands and a repressive system of taxation and forced labour. 'I know the tribes of Africa,' von Trotha told Leutwein. 'They are all alike. They only respond to force. It was and is my policy to use force with terrorism and even brutality. I shall annihilate the revolting tribes with streams of blood. Only after a complete uprooting will something emerge.'

Massive reinforcements were hastily prepared and dispatched. By July there were 5000 men to deal with a tribe which Leutwein estimated had only 2500 rifles and limited supplies of ammunition. The war had turned against the Hereros and they began to incur steady and damaging casualties. By early August they had been driven by the German onslaught to the foot of the Waterberg, east of Namibia's central plateau. Trotha saw his opportunity. He all but surrounded the sandstone massif with 4000 men, equipped with three machine guns and 32 cannons; on 11 August 1904; the battle of Waterberg began.

The Herero women accompanied their men into battle and sought to embolden them with wild ululating and shrieks of 'Who owns Hereroland? We own Hereroland!', and it was the women who carried the dead and wounded from the field. The Germans countered with a co-ordinated attack and their artillery took a terrible toll of the densely packed rear echelon where more than 50,000 men, women and children were compressed into a rectangle eight kilometres wide and sixteen kilometres long. By nightfall Samuel and his chiefs realised that further resistance was futile and gave orders to break out at any cost. The panic-stricken Herero masses followed the line of least resistance – to the south-east, into the waterless Omaheke Desert.

The scenes of carnage in the Herero camp were appalling. One German soldier wrote, of what confronted him: 'The death-rattle of the dying and the shrieks of the mad ... they echo in the sublime stillness of infinity.' Another soldier recalled, 'The scene which will be forever in my memory. For several kilometres along the Hamakari there were camps which had a short time before provided shelter for many thousands of men and cattle. Whatever was within range of our guns had been destroyed and everywhere there were signs of wild panicky flight. In the lean-tos cowered old men and women and children who had been left behind. The wounded, sick and dying awaited their fate crouched in corners. Everywhere there were numerous cattle left behind in their haste – and cattle are sacred to the Hereros – as evidence of the hysterical flight. Wagons filled with goods, furs, household items, apparently readied for flight, had been left behind. Numerous blankets, jewellery, whole cases of feathers were strewn about ... the whole national wealth of the Hereros lay on those roads ... The General forbade the killing of women and children but all armed men who were captured soon met their fate. A fearful punishment rained down on the Hereros; they will never recover from it.' The peace of the graveyard settled over the Waterberg.

Those Hereros that managed to break out were frantically digging in the deep Kalahari sands for water – pits as deep as twelve metres were later discovered. Uninterrupted pursuit by German patrols harried and broke up the clans still further. In the words of the official report: 'This bold enterprise shows up in the most brilliant light the ruthless energy of the German command in pursuing their beaten enemy. No pain, no sacrifice was spared in eliminating the last remnants of enemy resistance. Like a wounded beast the enemy was tracked down from one waterhole to the next, until finally he became the victim of his own environment. The arid Omaheke was to complete what the German army had begun: the extermination of the Herero nation.'

Of those who fled into the Kalahari about 1500 emerged in British Bechuanaland (Botswana) – an unknown number having died in the desert. But Trotha failed to end the war with the extermination of the Herero, as he had planned. Elements of the

*Right: A San Bushman woman in Sesfontein – perhaps the last surviving 'Strandloper' (a beachcombing people that were exterminated by Hottentots, Bantu and Europeans)*

refugee tribe managed to survive in the desert under even the most desperate conditions and they began filtering back into their homelands. In view of this, von Trotha issued a proclamation 'to the Herero nation' declaring: 'The Herero are no longer German subjects. They have murdered and plundered. They have hacked off ears, noses and other organs from wounded soldiers. Now, out of cowardice, they want to give up the fight ... The Herero nation must leave the country. If it will not do so I shall compel it by force. Inside German territory every Herero tribesman, armed or unarmed, with or without cattle, will be shot. No women and children will be allowed in the territory: they will be driven back to their people or fired on. These are the last words to the Herero nation from me, the great General of the mighty German Emperor.'

To enforce his decree the 'great General' placed a price on the heads of the Herero chiefs and made his soldiers eligible for blood money, although women and children were not to be directly fired upon, only chased back by shooting over their heads. 'This,' von Trotha explained, 'would mean that no male prisoners would be taken but also that no atrocities would take place towards women and children ... Our forces will not forget the reputation of the German soldier.' But outrage at the brutality of the draconian measures was growing. A withering repudiation of von Trotha's military dictatorship was spearheaded by Governor Leutwein, together with a section of the German population, the missionaries and the Colonial Department. An order countermanding von Trotha's proclamation declared that Kaiser Wilhelm 'would exercise clemency' towards those Hereros who gave themselves up voluntarily. Eventually 14,000 Hereros arrived at special camps set up by the Rhenish Mission.

When an armistice was signed on 20 December 1905 there were only about 16,000 survivors from a Herero population estimated at 80,000. Between 75 and 80 percent of the nation had perished. Though casualty figures are notoriously inaccurate, the total dead was probably greater than in the Boer War. Yet in their scramble for colonies, the Reichstag did not consider the slaughter of tens of thousands of Africans, the deaths of 2000 of their own soldiers and the expenditure of half a billion marks too high a price to pay. During this same period the Germans were carrying out repressions of a comparable savagery in East Africa, where, during the Maji-Maji rebellion, they made a point of executing the eldest son of every family in the region, and at least 100,000 Africans died without dignity or purpose.

In the aftermath of the war, the military colonial rulers saw it as their task 'to divest the Herero as far as possible of their national characteristics and gradually merge them with the other native groups into a single coloured working-class.' Deputy Governor Tecklenburg concluded that white rule would be permanently assured only if the Africans submitted emotionally as well as militarily: 'Every tribal organisation will cease. Werfs (villages) deep in the bush which try to avoid political supervision will not be tolerated. They would provide focal points for memories of tribal life and days when Africans owned land.' It was the first German attempt at implementing a 'final solution' to what was perceived as a purely racial problem. The tyrannous phraseology, the pernicous dialectic, the speaking of the unspeakable and the bloodshed itself – all would be echoed thirty years later by the countrymen of South West Africa's colonial masters.

Viewed in historical perspective, the Herero War was unimportant to Germany, an incident in a short-lived imperial adventure, although from its ashes sprouted the seeds of future German totalitarianism. For the Hereros it was the most traumatic event they had ever experienced. Samuel Maherero, the wastrel turned patriot, escaped to Botswana and died in a foreign land as his father had predicted. The tribe's great struggle had ended in tragedy, its pitiful remnants disbanded and broken.

A few hundred refugees fled north into Damara territory south-west of Kamanjab and later, at the invitation of their close relatives the Himba, moved further north into Kaokoland. A gradual influx of Herero from the southern reserves to relatives in Kaokoland occurred after 1920, and today it is their offspring that live at Sesfontein and in the surrounding countryside.

Sesfontein's polyglot community is largely made up of the people and their children who came here seeking a haven or a last resting-place. While roaming the settlement's Damara quarter I happened across a very old woman sitting outside a thatch hut, in the weak winter sunshine, smoking a home-made metal pipe. Her deepset blind eyes were folded closed, her face puckered and corrugated with age; the skin of her arms was scaled as a bird's, and her hands with their long curved nails looked like talons. Made aware of my presence by the click of my camera, she fidgeted and rustled and made a small chirruping sound. She wore the turban and long floral robe favoured by the old-school Damara women but she was unmistakably Khoisan. I felt sure she was the last surviving pure-blooded Bushman, referred to by state ethnologist N.J. van Wermelo in a report he published in the 1950s. The woman in question had been married to a Damara and been born on the Skeleton Coast at the mouth of the Uniab, about seven days' walk south-west of Sesfontein. Based on no scientific evidence whatsoever, I was tempted to speculate that the old crone before me was a relic of a mysterious group of beach-wandering Bushmen, the so-called 'Strandlopers'. These primitive Stone Age people had built huts with whalebone frames; they hunted seals and collected shellfish along the coastline, as well as scavenging the carcasses of whales and anything else edible cast up by the tide. Their whale-ribbed huts can still be seen on the bleak coastline, but the people have long since gone.

According to Lawrence Green*, when he visited Sesfontein in 1951 he was told: 'There were only ten wild roving Strandlopers left on the desert plain between the oasis and the sea.' He reported that they called themselves Dauna-Daman – 'seaside people on a desert plain'. They could count up to two after which they used a word signifying many. He further noted that there had been much inbreeding between the Bushmen and the Damaras, the result being children taller and darker than the Bushman parent.

There has also been extensive mingling between the Nama and the Damaras and it is not unusual to meet a black-skinned Swartbooi with only the high cheekbones proclaiming his Nama ancestry. But when I was introduced to the headman of Sesfontein, Theophilus Havagab, I met a pure Nama. He had the rich apricot-coloured

* *Lords of the Last Frontier* (page 45), Howard Timmins 1952, Cape Town

complexion, the heart-shaped face with bold prominent cheekbones and the broad nose. His full lips were characteristically pale red and slightly everted; the epicanthic fold of his upper eyelid and almond-shaped eyes were features that had once given rise to the belief – now disproved by geneticists – that the Khoisan were an outflung Mongolian tribe.

Elias had been raised in Sesfontein and, after our visit to the headman, he remarked, 'When I was a child the Hereros called the Namas *muhona* – they were powerful then but with their loss of power they have become degenerate. But that old Theophilus used to be a great hunter in his youth.'

Then Elias went on to tell me a story that has been enshrined in Sesfontein's folklore: 'In 1941, a few years before I was born, a stock-raiding male lion was caught in a gin-trap but only by the toes of his forepaw. Three Nama hunters, including Theophilus and the headman at that time, Husa Uichamab, followed up the lion. They came on it suddenly and their dog rushed at it recklessly. The enraged lion tore loose, pursued the dog around a tree before catching it and killing it. Husa fired his gun but missed and the lion then charged him; it knocked him down and straddled him, mauling him savagely and growling all the while. The poor man was nevertheless able to throw his rifle – the only firearm they had – to his companion, who grabbed it and fired but instead of dropping the lion, he shot dead the headman.

'It was later said that he did this on purpose so as to inherit the headman's stool [seat of power] but whether he was capable, in the heat of the moment, of such devilish plotting, seems hard to believe. [In old-world African villages, death by misadventure is never construed as such. It is always regarded as the result of witchcraft or premeditation.] At this point, Theophilus leapt onto the lion's back from behind, caught hold of its ears and tried to pull it off the headman, not realising he was dead. He screamed at the other man, "Shoot the lion!" The next shot pierced Theophilus's thigh, raked the breadth of the lion's chest, passed through its heart, and exited through Theophilus' other thigh. The lion was destroyed, the disgraced man who had shot Husa was denied his claim to the chieftaincy and Theophilus survived his gunshot and bite wounds to become Sesfontein's present headman. If you ask the old man he might even show you his scars from that encounter.'

I did not need to see the scars; I had seen something more poignant in the little hunter's unsqueamish gaze – an image of the past, a link with old Africa, its ancient and recent history, inexorably fading. For those who go to Sesfontein and have the eyes to see and an imagination to conjure with, who go with respect and an appreciation of what to look for, the signs are everywhere. In the high hills encircling the valley, there are elephant paths, about half a metre in width, that gradually converge on the springs. The paths have a remarkably even and smooth surface and are very well defined. They follow the easiest gradients and where they cross rocky outcrops, the boulders are polished by the traffic of hundreds of years. But the elephants have gone – most have been killed and the rest driven away.

The valley's once prosperous grass cover has been depleted by long years of occupation by African pastoralists and now, for much of the year, it is reduced to a dustbowl. Even the source of Sesfontein's wealth – its springs – has been undermined.

Left: *Theophilus Havagab, the Nama headman of Sesfontein*

In an ill-conceived attempt to increase the volume of water reaching the gardens, underground pipelines were installed which bypassed the giant winter thorns and sycamore figs that had been nourished by the springs. Today the centuries-old trees are all dead or dying. And the towering date palms, imported from Egypt and planted by the German garrison over eighty years ago, no longer bear fruit.

There was a tinge of the ominous in the African evening, as I stood in the thornscrub-invaded ruins of the German fort. It had been built with raw bricks and plaster to an impressive design – dominated by corner towers and turrets, with a large courtyard and adjoining camel stables. Since then the walls have been knocked down by locals saving themselves the effort of baking their own bricks, although a belated start has been made to safeguard its skeleton.

Night was falling in the shadows of the demolished outpost, beneath the palm's dark umbrella plumes. In the dying light, the dying wild figs and the raised click-tongued voices of a dying race, all spoke of the death of an epoch.

We camped that night on the short-grass alluvial plains abutting the Hoanib. The flatland prospect was irregularly decorated with big buckled mopanes and wide-branching camel thorns; the high-ranging cliffs demarcating the river course's northern flank looked dense and impenetrable. At dawn, as the first colours touched the land – deep green and minted gold, then the mountain's pinks and blues – there came a barrage of bird calls. It was a strident awakening – first crowned plovers protesting our presence, then red-billed hornbills, red-billed francolins, a grey lourie and a late calling pearl-spotted owl. A laughing dove murmured soft apologies.

After coffee and biscuits we drove to a wind-pump on the Ganamub River, which is a tributary of the Hoanib, so that Garth could confer with an auxiliary game scout he has stationed there. The wind-pump had been broken by elephants but the auxiliary, Abraham Tjavara, confirmed what an aerial survey had already revealed, that the elephants drinking there had moved north to the Hoarusib River. Abraham's dependants – two wives, ten children of his own and six of a deceased brother – sat watching us listlessly. Abraham complained of the hard times and the difficulty of providing for so many. To make matters worse, another brother was visiting from Opuwa in central Kaokoland, and had filled Abraham's head with horror stories. Apparently a group of Swapo insurgents had crossed the Kunene River and abducted a village of Tjimbas back to Angola, shooting six of them dead when they refused to go. Now Abraham wanted another man to join him, to improve their defences. Because of the lack of funds, as much as anything else, his request was out of the question and all Garth could do was seek to reassure him.

From Ganamub we headed south across the tawny Giribes Plains. Strange circular sandy patches, from three to six metres in diameter and completely devoid of vegetation, pockmarked the grasslands. Although thorough investigation included microbiological soil analysis, no explanation for the phenomenon has yet been arrived at, and although the patches have been shown to inhibit the growth of grass, the theory that the soil has been poisoned by decomposing euphorbias is still unproved.

We travelled under a hot bright blue sky, flanked by rock walls that narrowed and led us into the ill-defined bed of the Obias River, which quickly cut down through the hills to join the Hoanib. Earlier we had seen scattered rhino dung, and a pair of lappet-faced vultures had risen from their nest in the crown of a stunted camel thorn. There had been ground squirrels, but, except for a lone springbok ram that bolted across our bows with the terror-inspired speed of a hunted animal, we saw no other mammals, nor was there much sign to indicate they had ever been there.

The Hoanib forged westwards between great schist cliffs; majestic winter and umbrella thorns thrived in the fine sedimentary soil blown into the riverbed from the neighbouring desert. At the junction with the Mudorib River we flushed three cock ostriches that sprinted at high speed ahead of the Land Rover; we were unable to get ahead of them and they kept up for kilometre after kilometre, displaying heroic stamina. At last, at a point where the riverbed widened, we managed to speed past them and as we drew away they stopped running to stare after us, rapidly panting to dissipate their heat loads.

Soon we had left behind all signs of mankind and the further west we drove the more wildlife we encountered. Being so close to the protection of the Skeleton Coast Park, the gemsbok and giraffe were unfamiliarly tame. A steenbok gazed at us in astonishment before wheeling to scamper away. The wildlife was dependent on the food, water and shade provided by the Hoanib. Beyond the wind-swept river banks the vast, barren, remorseless Namib Desert spreads away, its spare life forms at the limit of existence.

The Namib – a Nama word meaning 'desert' – is set in earth colours, the greys, browns, reds and whites of the wind-blasted sand, gravel, rock and crusted salt from which it is fashioned. The colours subtly shift with the arc of the sun as it floats across a pale sky, undisturbed by clouds, that seems without end. Its bleakness is in dramatic contrast to the Hoanib's fertile sanctuary.

Throughout the afternoon a hot dry easterly – derived from anticyclones over the interior – whipped up a stinging sandstorm. A small herd of springbok stood exposed on the edge of the desert, hunched against the bombardment. At this time of the year the air is so full of dust that it becomes a feature of living there – nostrils and throat are always clogged, hair always stiff with static electricity. Towards the bitter end of winter when the land is at its driest, the sky is choked by a high-standing blanket of dust particles that is so dense it extinguishes the sun, so that it appears as if sunset has taken place in the mid-afternoon. The rest of the day, until true sunset, lingers on as a weird, rosy twilight.

At the foot of a ten metre-high river bank we came upon the hyena-rended carcass of an elephant that had fallen to its death. 'Probably stampeded by a low-flying aeroplane,' Garth surmised. 'That kind of inconsiderate behaviour is having a severely detrimental effect on the already traumatised elephant population, to the extent that it may be disrupting their breeding cycles. But it's impossible to control the few irresponsible pilots involved. All we can do is make public appeals and hope for the best.'

Far out in the desert, three giraffes drifted across a stark lunar landscape glazed pale purple by the waning sun. They appeared to float above the hard edge of the horizon,

Overleaf: *Springbok ram in the dry dunes abutting the Uniab River, Skeleton Coast*

hesitated there a moment, then disappeared so suddenly they might have been an illusion. Jackals howled to hurry in the night. A dull copper-red sun settled through the dust haze, bringing an umbrella thorn into gnarled silhouette. Around a campfire, savouring a bowl of goat stew, I watched as a crescent moon dropped, till only the tips of its horns showed above the horizon and then were gone. A dove muttered in its sleep.

Morning came with the racketing of red-billed francolins, their wild cries cracking the still air. The sun swam up into an orange sky and its track burnt black an immature martial eagle coasting above the darkly silent tree-line. The wind had turned and we had not travelled far when a sudden blast of cold air announced the ocean's proximity. The change in temperature was like hitting a wall – one moment the air was scorched, the next bitingly chilled. Then we broke out of the riverbed and into a broad flood plain where the Hoanib's seasonal spate banks up against a ten kilometre wide dune belt. The floor of the flood plain was overgrown with tamarisks and salsola. Flood waters promote the growth of nutritious annual grasses, and a sorghum grass that grows three metres tall, which elephants are very partial to. When conditions are right, with surface water still available, the Hoanib elephants base themselves in the floodplain – but the dry season was already well advanced by the time we arrived there; the pools had evaporated and the elephants moved on.

Out in the open, a jackal lay curled to ward off the nip in the wind. It raised its head, regarding us with apparent unconcern, as we made a close approach. The early morning sun reflected bright points of light in its liquid amber eyes. But at some stage we crossed an invisible line and the jackal's nerve broke – it came to its feet, turned and trotted away in one fluid motion. Further along we found fresh hyena spoor and the tracks of two lions that led from the flood plain straight out into the desert. Handsome augur buzzards perched on guano-splashed rocky outcrops that overlooked the bottomlands. One, leisurely riding a thermal, was furiously mobbed by a pair of rock kestrels.

Only very rarely, in years of exceptional rainfall, does the Hoanib force a passage through the shifting sand dunes and break through to the sea. More usually, the water ebbs away into the sand to continue its journey by the tedious process of subterranean diffusion. Seepage of the Hoanib's sweet waters over the last stretch to the coast – a passage which may last for years – takes place over a wide underground deltaic area. Living proof of this hidden percolation is found in the rich birdlife at the miraculous Hoanib Oasis in the heart of the dunes and again at its estuary.

In the desert, where the struggle for survival is desperate, an astonishing range of adaptations have emerged to cope with the inhospitable conditions. On the crest of a dune, near the Hoanib Oasis, we had the good fortune to meet up with three lions that had made bird meat the mainstay of their diet. The well-adjusted predators prey on the flocks of cormorants and flamingos that roost by night at the oasis – charging into the midst of the sleeping birds and knocking down as many as possible before they take to flight. There are other lions that patrol the beaches to pounce on unsuspecting seals, and who compete with brown hyenas for carrion washed ashore. In very arid environments animals tend to be opportunistic, general feeders and there are very few desert-dwelling carnivores that will not resort to alternative nourishment when necessary. The limited food resources severely restricts the number of lions living on the Skeleton Coast, but those that have made their home in this most unlikely of environments are apparently thriving and cubs have been successfully reared.

The inauspiciously named Skeleton Coast lies in the northern reaches of the Namib, that long coastal desert stretching from the Olifant's River in South Africa to north of Mogamedes in Angola, some 2000 kilometres in extent. The Namib belongs to that select five percent of the earth's land surface classified as 'extremely arid'. Its antiquity is prodigious; the Namib tract dates back to the Cretaceous and has not experienced climates significantly more humid than semi-arid for any length of time during the last 80 million years. Full development of the Benguela Current and its associated cold upwelling system accentuated the desert conditions during the Late Tertiary. The Benguela Current is driven by giant oceanic convection systems thousands of kilometres from its source in the icy Antarctic Ocean, up the west coast of southern Africa to the equator. This mighty stream of nutrient-rich water is encouraged to rise to the surface by prevailing winds. The cold offshore ocean and the south-westerly sea breeze are too cool to bear moisture in sufficient quantity for rain clouds to form. The rare rainfalls that occur are the result of clouds crossing the breadth of the subcontinent from the Indian Ocean.

Despite the absence of rain from the Atlantic seaboard, moisture does manage to penetrate in the form of fogs, when air in contact with the frigid ocean is chilled to saturation point. Sea breezes carry the life-giving water vapour into the heart of the Namib, bringing relief from high temperatures and low humidities, and contributing to the unique character of the desert ecosystem.

The Skeleton Coast's sinister reputation is well deserved. No-one knows how many ships have been driven through banks of fog by gales and treacherous currents to destruction on uncharted reefs. The splintered coastline of rocks and sand has, for centuries, been a place where men and ships came ashore to die, as did seals and whales, and the coast's name probably derives from the accumulation of their petrified bones.

The explorer Charles Anderrson, never one to minimize the vileness of his surroundings, lamented: 'When a heavy sea-fog rests on these uncouth and rugged surfaces – and it does so very often – a place fitter to represent the infernal regions could scarcely, in searching the world round, be found. A shudder, amounting almost to fear, came over me when its frightful desolation first suddenly broke upon my view. "Death," I exclaimed, "would be preferable to banishment to such a country".'

At its mouth, the Hoanib gives rise to a small brackish lagoon that is frequented by parties of flamingos, a few of which stood idly along the seashore; the fresh pink of their plumage contrasted prettily with the ocean's deep blue, and restored sharpness to their sombre, amorphous world. Jackals patrolled the beaches – lean, furtive, black-backed rustlers, with a practised eye always levelled at the main chance.

That night the roll of the cold Atlantic breakers set up a constant primordial resonance that was overlaid by the harsh querulous gobbling of cormorants nesting on abandoned mine gantries. The cormorants – itinerant diurnal fishermen and natives of the shoreline – return each evening, in low jagged columns, to sleep in their familiar

festering eyries. Their comings and goings are regulated by the vicissitudes of the weather. On misty, damp mornings they hang back, reluctant to go to work, irritably exchanging points of view like old merchant traders in a Middle East bazaar. But on clear mornings they are gone, as silent and composed as a commando on alert – a scourge to fish shoals and very good at their business. When fish in any numbers are encountered the cormorants circle, sight them in, then commence to dive with cool precision, throwing up splashes of spume, and rising up again till they are gorged. Once satiated they settle on the nearest convenient site – a wrecked ship serves admirably – to comment on the day's fishing and to preen their sodden feathers.

The next day dawned slowly, a grey sunrise on grey water; a cold silver light. The air was calm and clammy; there was an absence of sound except for the dull boom of the surf and the wild cries of seabirds. In that enveloping eeriness was the echo of cataclysm – no wonder the early mariners, believing in a flat earth as they had, feared that on reaching the Skeleton Coast they had come to the end of the world.

Left: *Greater flamingos on the Skeleton Coast, at the mouth of the Hoanib River*

CHAPTER

# 7

# Kaokoland: Northwards

The Kaokoland trip, when it finally came about, was made in the best traditions and spirit of exploratory travel, where the point of the odyssey is the journey, not the destination. 'I'm really looking forward to this,' Garth had said with quiet enthusiasm. 'If the security situation permits, we'll be visiting parts I haven't seen in at least thirteen years – even then I only travelled them lightly. Where we go will depend on how active Swapo is; that's something I'll check with the police commandant. I'd like to go north of Opuwa, all the way to the Marienfluss – right into the heart of Himba country.'

We set out from Wêreldsend on a rough track that meanders northwards across plains rubbled with solidified magma and dotted with welwitschias, their wind-shredded tentacle-like leaves making them look like a prehistoric species of terrestial octopus. Elias, riding in the open back of the Land Rover, would occasionally tap on the cab roof to draw our attention to points of interest – ten gemsbok, about a kilometre away, standing on the saddle connecting two hills; a lone kudu bull chewing with relish the succulent tips of the toxic *Euphorbia damarana*; a pair of giraffe, stark as killed trees, come to a standstill on a barren prairie so wide it seemed without end. 'Giraffe have disappeared from all the inhabited areas of Damaraland and Kaokoland,' Garth commented. 'Most of them were run down by hunters on horseback. Giraffe are so easy to hunt; gemsbok and kudu at least have a chance, but giraffe are soft targets.'

No doubt preoccupied with the war situation in Kaokoland, Garth had, consciously or not, reverted to the military jargon he had used in Rhodesia during the bloody years leading up to that country's independence. 'Soft target' more usually refers to the relatively vulnerable civilian objectives on which the insurgents had often concentrated their attacks. Earlier, Garth had spoken of obtaining a 'sit rep' – a situation report – on the routes we intended travelling, and now he passed along some of the precautions he had developed during the period he had worked as a range ecologist on a cattle and game ranch in the south-east of Rhodesia, during the height of the guerilla war: 'Don't let the locals know where you intend camping that night, there might be "terr" sympathisers among them. Eat early and doss down about a hundred metres from your vehicle, which is an obvious target for a mortar or rocket attack. Avoid obvious routes, and don't exit by the same track you came in on – dissidents are liable to lay a land-mine a few kilometres from your camp-site. For the most part mines are not laid indiscriminately – particular targets are zeroed-in on. If the target misses the mine, the layers will very probably dig it up again for use elsewhere. Another basic precaution: when walking, maintain at least five metres between individuals, and always go armed. Unarmed people present the soft targets that "terrs" thrive on. People tend not to take sufficient care until the war gets close to them. When I saw the body of a neighbour, who was also one of my best friends, I not only felt a great sense of loss but realised that it could just as easily have been me that was killed in that ambush.'

Garth shook his head sorrowfully, remembering the waste and bitterness the racial war had engendered. 'Five white staff members and thirty black labourers were killed by "terrs", and a further thirteen whites were killed on surrounding farms. I took over a section where the previous manager had been ambushed and wounded and his African assistant killed. Within the first three months of arriving, my office and store-room were burned down; but then, probably as a result of my good relations with the African staff, things started improving. June played an important role, putting her nursing experience to good use by maintaining the only clinic in the area. By that stage of the war, the local government clinics had been closed down. Some of June's patients had walked or been carried for more than forty kilometres. She successfully treated some pretty serious cases too,' he went on, with obvious pride in his wife's achievements under extremely difficult circumstances. 'I established labour committees through which the staff could voice grievances, and which assumed much of the responsibility for upholding discipline. But one thing we were never able to get under control was the stock thefts, which continued on an enormous scale.'

Out there, in the peace and solitude, with the insistent whimpers of Namaqua sandgrouse sounding overhead, the war seemed very far away. This is how it must have been, I thought, on countless occasions just before the firing started. I had made several trips into UDI Rhodesia and been astonished at the air of unreality about it all. There was a façade of normality, composure even, behind which acts of unspeakable violence had daily been perpetrated by both sides.

'I had one very interesting experience,' Garth went on. 'It was a common practice amongst Zanla – the military wing of Zanu, Mugabe's largely Shona party – to hold trials, with labourers as witnesses, to determine whether white managers were "enemies of the people". Well, I must have featured at one of those trials and escaped the death sentence, I guess, because my Shona assistant led me straight into an ambush one day which would have been the end of me if that had been their intention. But it turned out they only wanted to talk. The group leader proposed a sort of mutual non-aggression pact, whereby they would leave me alone if I turned a blind eye to their movements through the ranch. They also asked for a gift – they suggested denim jeans – as a token of my goodwill. They were quite reasonable and accepted it when I told them I would have to think about it. As a South African I had gone to Rhodesia determined not to take sides in the civil war, but by the latter stages of the conflict neutrality was simply no longer possible. When that friend of mine got killed a few

Overleaf: *Springbok rams jousting*

weeks later, I let it be known that any understanding between the guerillas and myself was out of the question. As it turned out, about a year after this another ambush was set for me. This time they meant business. June and the kids were also in the truck and we only escaped by sheer chance. That was the final straw and I decided to pack it in. And now here I am, heading back to Kaokoland just as things are hotting up there.'

On the crisp, dry air, the rich melodious prattling of the innumerable Stark's larks carried with uncompromising clarity. We were following a barely discernible torrent course and Garth remarked, 'I always expect to see rhino in this sort of terrain. They love to lie-up in a dry wash, next to a *Euphorbia damarana* – then they jump up when you drive past, confused and frightened and very bad tempered.' We stayed with the water course until it dissolved into the barren plains, without encountering a rhino, although we did see four gemsbok that cantered away, kicking up dust, then stopping to stare back over their shoulders at us.

Below a shadowed Ecke mountain a family group of mountain zebra – a stallion, three mares and a foal – stood poised for flight, giving vent to their alarm with strange little whickers. Their muted vocabulary is in marked contrast to the wild rallying barks of their plains cousins. They are further distinguished by the small dewlaps at their throats, the lack of shadow stripes, and by the narrow transverse stripes that run across the rump to form a grid iron pattern. They are adapted to life in rocky, mountainous regions – so much so that when some were forced, by the drought, to move into the eastern sandveld, their hooves, no longer worn down by the stony substrate, kept on growing and curled up to resemble Turkish slippers.

We camped that night in the dry bed of the Aub River, beside the bleached, scattered bones of a poached rhino. The monumental mass of a dead leadwood tree, as compacted as ancient masonry, stood like a cenotaph over the remains. On a pre-dinner stroll down the Aub, Garth noted with satisfaction increased signs of elephant occupancy. Not that we saw any elephants, indeed the only mammal we met with was an elephant shrew, that turned its large-eared head to regard us with bright eyes, its long snout seeming to tremble with indignation at our intrusion. The primitive mouse-sized little creature is a voracious diurnal predator of invertebrates, spending eighty per-cent of its day catching and eating a weight of insects, snails, millipedes and worms equivalent to its own. Their order is endemic to Africa and the five genera are widely distributed over the continent, some species preferring broken, semi-arid areas, while others nose through fallen leaves on humid forest floors. Galvanised by the sudden hysterical racketeing from a foraging party of bare-cheeked babblers, the elephant shrew bounded away on long hind legs, its slender tail held erect, at a great turn of speed.

To the south-east, burgeoning cumulus rimmed the horizon, but the sky above was clear of clouds. That rain had fallen in the area was apparent from the numerous puddles, and the unseasonal localised shower had left the air dense with moisture. Soon after sunset a heavy dew began to settle, an extraordinary occurrence at this time of the year, when the climate is usually so arid it shrivels an orange within a matter of days. As if as surprised as we were by the aberrant weather, a double-banded sandgrouse exclaimed musically, just once, then fell silent. An insomniac turtle dove, troubled by the silence, filled the vacuum by repeating a harsh, throaty 'coo' over and over again.

From out of the night, a fearsome, some might say loathsome-looking solifuge scuttled with bewildering speed into the light cast by the camp-fire and fetched-up against my sandalled foot, cautiously examining it with long pedipalps held forward as feelers. I knew that it lacked poison glands and meant me no harm, but its large, spider-like appearance and massive jaws were nonetheless disconcerting. It required a great effort of will to hold my foot still, but, after a cursory probe, the miniature monster zipped off suddenly in another direction.

Solifuges are popularly referred to as 'sun spiders', which is a complete misnomer, for not only are most species nocturnal but, despite a superficial resemblance to spiders, they belong to a totally different group. Our visitor might have been attracted to the insects, themselves attracted by the camp-fire, but it might just as likely have been merely passing through, as their hunting technique seems to consist of high speed random movements in search of prey. Insects are held by sucker-like discs on the tips of the solifuge's pedipalps, and passed through its jaws until the body contents are extracted. Although not poisonous, those jaws can deliver a powerful bite, and I said to Garth, only half-jokingly, 'I hope the damned thing doesn't get into my sleeping bag' – it had been heading in that direction when I lost sight of it.

'No need to worry,' he replied. 'All those sorts of creatures are reluctant to walk on a groundsheet.' I had heard that story before, and naively believed it, until one night I had nearly stepped, barefoot, on a highly venomous *Parabuthus* scorpion that was obviously not familiar with that particular piece of bushlore and had made itself at home on my tent's groundsheet. I told Garth of my experience and he grinned slyly. 'Oh well, nothing's perfect. Even if it's not true, belief in its efficacy gives newcomers to the bush a bit of piece of mind.'

I know lamentably little about invertebrates, nor do I have a way with them. Years ago I accompanied a safari party into the bush, ostensibly as their guide, and they appeared to have faith in me. Around the camp-fire one night, an armoured beetle came winging in from the dark and landed amongst us, flat on its back, legs helplessly groping the air. The tourists enquired as to what kind it was – I didn't know but thought I could brazen it out. 'Let's take a closer look,' I airily suggested, and picked it up, whereupon it plunged its pincers into my finger. The pain was acute, but the embarrassment of having to admit that I had not anticipated its reaction would have been more so. Instead I held up my hand, with the beetle imbedded in the tip of my finger, for their inspection. 'Doesn't it hurt?' a concerned lady asked. 'Not really,' I replied. 'These fellows are alright as long as they have something to hold on to' – still gamely pretending I knew what it was I was dealing with. Since then I have become a lot more careful about handling strange insects, and a lot less reticent about acknowledging my ignorance of them.

A gusting overnight wind had dispersed any lingering rainclouds, and we set off next morning in a soft autumnal light. I had taken Elias's position in the rear and as we slowly picked our way down the river course, I looked up to see a high-flying jet describe a sharp, white vapour trail across the inverted blue bowl of the upper stratosphere. I wondered what its Europe-bound passengers made of the featureless immensity of arid savanna Africa, as it unfolded beneath them.

We hadn't gone far when Garth braked to a halt and, jumping from the cab, asked, 'Did you see that?'; then answered his own question: 'Fresh rhino spoor'. He sat on his heels to scrutinize the big three-toed tracks that plodded with ponderous self-assurance down the middle of the sandy bed. In lieu of a ruler, Garth cut a straw to the precise width of the hind print and would later compare its dimensions to those already recorded in his catalogue. 'A big bull,' Garth said, nodding approvingly. We continued down the river in the rhino's wake, noting where it had stopped to browse, using its molars to cut off acacia and grewia twigs with surgical neatness. The tracks eventually led into a thicket and boulder-choked crevice that proved impassable for the vehicle, and we were forced out of the riverbed. As it now seemed unlikely we would ever come up with the rhino, we abandoned the idea and went on our way.

Much of our route had taken us straight cross-country, often without benefit of even a rudimentary track. During the course of our travels together, Garth had shown himself to be not only a first class field mechanic, but a bush driver of rare ability. To minimize the jolts and grinding protests of the car requires a certain deftness, and the skill, born of experience, to correctly 'read' the way ahead. Garth drove through sand and broken country – ceaselessly gear shifting, easing over rocks and potholes – in two wheel drive without incident. 'It saves a little on petrol,' he commented, 'and it's reassuring to know that if I ever get into trouble I've got the four wheel capability to fall back on.'

Eventually we joined the gravel national road, and stayed with it until we reached the veterinary checkpoint at Werda, which is also the doorway to the war zone. We would be travelling the 'white road' – so-called because it is surfaced with blinding white calcrete gravel – and Garth made a point of checking at the police post whether there was any likelihood of trouble ahead. 'The sergeant was reassuring,' he said when he got back. 'There are no problems as far as they know. They've given the white road a clean bill of health – so far there haven't been any incidents this year.'

North of Werda, at Otjitjekwa, we left the main Ruacana road to branch westwards towards Opuwa, and a short way along we were hailed by two horse-riding Hereros, who had recognised our vehicle. What they had to tell us made an interesting tail-piece to the Ombonde giraffe poaching incident. The older of the two men said that it had been his horse that was used to run down the giraffe, although he claimed he had had no idea at the time what Adam intended to do with it. Only later did he find out, when – he confided with a sheepish grin – he was rewarded with some of the dried giraffe meat. He went on to say that the local Hereros had been outraged by the 'injustice' of the trial. They maintained that Chris had been 'sent' by Adam to kill the giraffe, and as a younger man had had no choice but to obey. Nonetheless, he had been found as guilty as Adam and sentenced to equal punishment. The court's verdict had directly contravened traditional Herero law as regards culpability. Chris's indignant relatives had petitioned their headman, Keefas Muzuma, who upheld their appeal and instructed Adam to pay

Right: *Three generations of Himba in typical daub and sapling hut*

Chris's fine; a judgement that Adam apparently accepted without demur.

Both the horsemen carried old World War II .303 rifles, as do a considerable proportion of Kaokoland's adult male tribesmen. When, in the early 1980s, Swapo extended its activities into Kaokoland, the security forces began a programme of arming the civilian population to act as an informal army aginst the insurgents and, according to their own estimates, more than three thousand rifles were issued. Whatever the intention, the guns have, in reality, been turned on the wildlife and a dreadful slaughter has taken place. Because of the over-riding precedence of waging a war, nature conservation has been relegated to a pitifully low priority. Authorities are afraid that to enforce anti-poaching measures would alienate the tribes and drive them into Swapo's embrace.

Kaokoland's agony is a recent development in a vicious festering bush war, that has consumed the whole of northern Namibia. It ignited nineteen years ago, in August 1966, when the police base camp at Ongulumbashe was attacked by members of PLAN – the People's Liberation Army of Namibia, the military wing of SWAPO, the South West African People's Organisation. The attack was beaten off but the stage was set for a slow build-up of the South African Defence Force (SADF), to the point where today there is a sizeable army massed along the Angolan border, at a cost of at least 1.5 million rand a day. In a struggle that neither side is close to winning, hundreds of young South Africans have lost their lives as well as thousands of Namibians.

In the early stages of the war, when the Portuguese colonial empire was still intact, Swapo was able to do little more than conduct hit-and-run operations, and campaigns of rural politicisation. However, with the demise of the Portuguese government under the weight of its colonial wars in April 1974, a new chapter, fraught with regional and international implications, was opened. In attempting to ensure a 'friendly' regime – that of Jonas Savimbi's Unita Faction – in the newly independent Angolan capital of Luanda, and with the encouragement of the then American Secretary of State, Henry Kissinger, three South African armoured columns crossed into Angola in August 1975, and reached almost as far north as the capital. The desperate MPLA government in Luanda called on the assistance of Cuban troops, which were speedily dispatched and today number between 20,000 and 30,000. In response, the South Africans appealed for American assistance, but none was forthcoming and, in March the following year, they were forced to retreat back into Namibia. As a consequence, Swapo was now able to establish bases near the Angolan border and to intensify its guerilla war.

In the succeeding years, Swapo took advantage of the rainy season to launch assaults, aimed primarily at gaining recruits and infiltrating the white farming areas south of Ovamboland. Each raid was met by the South African army – arguably the strongest defence force on the continent – and was smashed into the mud. Swapo's lack of military success has prompted some observers to dismiss it as the most ineffective guerilla movement in the Third World, but despite their battering Swapo refuses to disappear, doggedly rallying its forces – estimated at about 6000 – in preparation for another assault.

The South African security forces reacted with a policy of 'pro-active defence', based on the age-old principle of buffer territory. In 1977 the SADF went beyond their limited 'pre-emptive strikes' and 'hot pursuits', with a decision to take the war back into southern Angola. A strike, code-named Operation Rheindeer, was launched, ostensibly to take out Swapo bases and to protect Namibia's northern frontier. It was wholly successful. This was followed in 1978 by the attack on Kassinga, and in 1981 by Operation Protea, a major invasion aimed, among other objectives, at removing recently installed Sovient Sam missile sites. Protea represented a dramatic new development in the war. Supported by repeated air strikes, four large motorised columns of South African troops engaged Angolan army units in Xangongo and Ongiva, fighting pitched battles up to two hundred kilometres inside Kunene province. That offensive established South African military supremacy over much of southern Angola, partly through the agency of Jonas Savimbi's Unita forces. At the time of writing, the SADF was pulling out of southern Angola, on the understanding that the MPLA government denies Swapo the right to launch raids from its territory. The signs are that South Africa intends to disengage from Namibia in the not-too-distant future, but should the current peace initiatives fail, all that remains is increasing polarisation.

Swapo started to infiltrate Kaokoland in February 1980, at a time when security surveillance was very low. The incursion was somewhat baffling, as the region has no tactical or strategic targets, and could only have been aimed at stretching the South African Armed Force's supply lines. At the same time they probably sought to politicise the locals, while pursuing the conventional guerilla tactics of limited attacks against military installations and the mining of roads. Kaokoland's rugged terrain ideally suited their hit-and-run strategy, permitting them to escape into the northern mountains, which are inaccessible to vehicles. On foot, the guerillas – fit, fast and prepared to live under the roughest conditions – had the advantage. By the time I arrived however, the territory was relatively quiet and news reports suggested that Swapo had switched its thrust eastwards, into Kavango, thus extending the security force's strength along almost the entire length of Namibia's northern border.

'When I last came up here, two years ago, this area was a "hot" road,' Garth said. 'It's still "warm". I doubt whether anyone in Opuwa would drive down here without a mineproof vehicle.' As our Land Rover was not mineproof, that last piece of information stimulated an unpleasant groin-tingling sensation, that was only exacerbated when a little further on, we came upon a burnt-out pick-up truck that had struck a landmine. A mangled enamel mug lay pathetically discarded beside the twisted wreck. 'Never knew what hit them,' Garth muttered.

We passed on from that scene of minor carnage in a very subdued frame of mind. Garth said, 'Travelling these rough roads, rocks are always being thrown up and they hit the undercarriage with a loud *crack*! Each time it happens I get a hell of a fright, but of course you don't hear the landmine you trip.'

We camped that night near the Otuzemba artesian spring, in an area where a single conservation-minded Herero headman, Werimba Rutjani, has steadfastly protected the wildlife within his ward. There is no doubt that his strong stand is the main reason why elephants and other game still occur here, while none at all survive in the surrounding districts.

The spring rises on high ground, behind which crouch dolomite hills emblazoned with two majestic baobabs, thrust up on the slopes like old roots of life. The open ground around the water was strewn with elephant dung. 'This spring used to be – probably still is – a good example of the many fountains in Kaokoland that I found to be peaceably shared by humans, their stock and elephants,' Garth said as we inspected the spring's perimeter for tracks. 'In the dry season these waters were used by hundreds of head of cattle during the day, then, an hour or two after sunset, the first elephants would arrive, with further herds coming to drink throughout the night. There was very little friction between man and elephant; each respected the drinking times of the other, and no reports were received of cattle being injured by elephants, as sometimes happens with rhinos.'

Irrigation furrows carried water to a mielie and tobacco garden a few hundred metres from the spring. The tilled land was protected from the elephants by meshed thorn branches, hung with rattling cans and an old cow bell. Desiccated zebra carcasses in the vicinity of the spring spoke of the drought's torment. That the local headman had managed to protect at least thirty elephants, as well as zebra and impala, at a time when his people were suffering great hardship, was little short of miraculous.

On a brief foot patrol in search of another spring which Garth knew existed nearby, we came upon the spoor of leopard, hyena, zebra and duiker, the dung middens of impala and an old elephant cadaver. We returned to our camp-site in the gathering dusk, to find that Elias had already built a fire, and as we emerged from the gloom of the tree-line he called to remind us that the hour of the elephant was rapidly approaching.

In the dark, double-banded sandgrouse twittered in to drink; a blacksmith plover scolded with harsh metallic clinking notes, like hammer blows on an anvil. During our meal Elias mentioned that we weren't far from another spring, Otjongombe, the Place of the Cattle, which was the exclusive preserve of the Hereros – any whites or Namas going there were certain to die. 'I'd like to visit that place,' I teased him. 'No, *muhona*, it's not a joke,' Elias insisted firmly. 'Some whites who tried to get there were only saved when their car got stuck in a riverbed. That was a warning; if they had not turned back as they did, they would have all perished.'

I found the Hereros' retention of their traditional beliefs and ancestor worship tremendously refreshing. In the early part of this century, those Hereros that had been evangelized blamed the calamities arising from the rinderpest epizootic, and the war with Germany, on their abandonment of the old ways, and so turned their backs on Christianity to rediscover their roots. The rejection of foreign influences has largely exempted the Hereros from the spiritual emptiness that besets most modern detribalised Africans, who have been taught to relinquish their cultures, yet are not accepted in the new world even when they have mastered its ways.

We turned in early, and I was still awake at nine o'clock when I heard a low growl, then the ruffling of water as the first elephants waded in to drink. By the light of a gibbous moon, I watched through binoculars as the great beasts detached themselves

Right: *An unmarried Himba woman, her marital status determined by her hairstyle*

from the anonymous darkness, to quietly gather around the spring. There appeared to be three herds, about twenty-five elephants in all, although there were only two calves. I assumed that the paucity of young animals stemmed – as it did in other parts of Kaokoland and Damaraland – from the effects of the drought.

The dark looming bulk of the elephants, their rumbling and watery gurgles, the *thuk* of the mud and water plastered on to parched flanks, the pale light reflecting off calcrete boulders, and the thin mopane scrub, all put me in mind of many similar evenings spent at the Ombika waterhole in Etosha. Then, as now, the adolescent bulls lingered after the others had departed, wrestling and sparring, their ivory clashing with loud hollow smacks. A juvenile broke from the group to playfully chase off a family of zebras that had drawn too close. A zebra squealed its frustration and the elephant blared a reply that split wide the night air.

Early the next morning a Herero, with four bony black dogs at his heel, came by our camp-site. The man was carrying a rifle, and explained that the previous evening one of the cattle had been mauled – he suspected a lion, and confirmed that there were still a few left in the district. He was hoping to track the culprit down but delayed the hunt long enough to accept our offer of a cup of coffee. Nodding at Garth, he asked; 'Don't you remember me? You came here about ten years ago and stayed for quite a long time. You used to catch snakes.' Garth's youthful snake-collecting avocation was obviously the one peculiarity the man recalled most vividly. Tribal Africans still regard anyone who handles live venomous reptiles with the awe usually reserved for those dealing in the supernatural.

At Werimba Rutjani's village we were shown the cow that had been attacked – its back had been deeply lacerated, and a bite on its thigh had left it with a dragging limp. Then we went on to an interview with old Werimba himself, and I asked what had motivated his singular crusade on behalf of wild animals. 'It does not seem strange to me, that I should protect the animals,' he replied gravely. 'I learnt to do so from my parents. The animals are not bad; if they go we would be exposed to a great loneliness of spirit. Where there are animals the land lives; without them the land begins to die. This is my farm and these animals are also mine. We like to see them, to live side by side with them. If we get hungry, maybe I will send a young man to Opuwa for a permit to shoot an old kudu bull. So far I have not done this. Even in the drought there was enough money to buy mielie-meal; it was not necessary to hunt. I have told my neighbours not to hunt here; I have also told the commissioner in Opuwa he may not hunt here.'

Garth pointed out that, in the old days, elephants had repeatedly damaged windpumps, either by rubbing against the structure or pulling it down, when for some reason it had stopped pumping water. Elephants also frequently raided the mielielands – didn't this make the people angry? 'What does it help to get angry?', Werimba replied without a trace of irony. 'The elephants still break into the gardens and they have damaged the dam at the wind-pump. When they do this we drive them away – these things belong to people, and the elephants have no right to them. But nor do we have the right to prevent the elephants from using the natural springs, or living in the veld as they have always done.'

Werimba may not have found his stance unusual, but I thought it remarkable in a land where practically everyone grabbed what they could from nature's declining windfall. 'Not many like him around,' Garth affirmed, as we drove on to Opuwa. 'I've suggested that the Trust provide the money to buy a heifer for the old man. Cattle are the most esteemed gift you can give a Herero, and it would be a fitting way to express our appreciation for his good work.'

We reached Opuwa (once spelt Ohopoho), Kaokoland's oppressive administrative centre, in the early afternoon. A high barbed wire security fence circled the dreary rows of prefabricated and blighted brick houses that lined dusty streets. Unattended flocks of goats wandered the lanes, scavenging amongst mouldering heaps of garbage. Men in police camouflage uniforms and military browns were everywhere, contrasting incongruously with the bare-torsoed Himbas and extravagantly robed Herero women, who gathered in groups to confer softly.

In the heat of the afternoon a drunken Himba, dressed in a stained khaki shirt, traditional leather apron and skin sandals, sprawled on the concrete floor of a liquor store, while the other customers stepped around him. Garth accepts the Himbas at their own evaluation, which is not low, and he was distressed by the mood of apathy and defeat that seemed to be enveloping many members of the tribe. 'Once they only visited this detested outpost of the twentieth century on brief trading forays, and left again as soon as they could,' he said. 'But the loss of their cattle during the drought, and the ripple effect of the war, has demoralised them. Now many of them get washed up here to stay, stripped of their possessions and their self-respect.'

On the outskirts of Opuwa, these rural refugees have erected dilapidated tin shanties and dung-and-mud humpies to create an overnight slum, where hygiene is basic and sanitation almost non-existent. Scrawny pullets scratched over bare dirt yards that have become open-air markets, with corn cobs and bloody chunks of meat proffered for sale. The sweet stench of rot permeated the baked tropical air.

The brooding harshness, the pervasive ugliness of Opuwa grimly reflected the realities of the war. In a grocery shop I queued behind an African who, Elias informed me, had had one entire side of his face badly burnt in a landmine incident. The scalding had puckered the skin, dragging his eye down and twisting the corner of his mouth into a horrible grimace. His disfigurement crudely symbolized everything the perverse fortified village of Opuwa represents. Its intrinsic ambience was that of a cinematic Mexican bandit town, where life is brutal and cheap. Whatever it started out as, Opuwa has become an aberration and an affront – a desperate outpost in the immense solitude of a hostile African plain.

We had arranged to meet up with Chris Eyre and Lucas Mpomporo in Opuwa, and found their Land Cruiser parked outside the police station. Chris had come north to take a statement from a convicted Herero poacher, who had earlier indicated his willingness to implicate a white Windhoek dealer as the end receiver for poached ivory and rhino horn. The poacher's uncle was the headman at Kaoko Otavi, and back in 1970, he had offered to sell rhino horn to Garth – clearly the family had been involved in the traffic of illegal game products for at least thirteen years, and probably for much longer than that.

Chris' would-be informer was an ex-special policeman from Kaoko Otavi, and he had hoped that this would ensure the man's co-operation. But when Chris strode from the police station, furiously sucking his pipe, he announced after a curt greeting: 'The bastard's clammed up. Says he never knew the identity of his buyer in Windhoek. Personally, I think he's been bribed. Well,' he added more quietly, and with a meaningful glance towards the station; 'the police are questioning him now. He'll come down to our camp-site later this evening and we'll see if they've helped to refresh his memory. It's so bloody frustrating. I know who he's been selling the stuff to but I can't get any evidence against him. It's becoming a personal vendetta. He knows I'm after him, and would dearly love to put him away, but he's so damned slippery. That fellow in there is really my only link, but I'm convinced that in return for his silence he's been promised a fat bonus when he gets out of gaol.'

On our way back to pick up Elias we bumped into Adam Tjikwara, dressed in the same disintegrating city best he had worn to his court appearance. Adam managed a weak smile when he saw us, and said he was in Opuwa to sell goats to help pay for his fine. He made no mention that he had been ruled responsible for his assistant's fine as well and, tactfully, neither did we.

We made camp in an acacia grove adjacent to the town, but screened from it by the stately wood of tall, well-spaced trees. Columns of goats and donkeys churned a dust haze as they were driven by, en route from pasturelands to corral. The sheltering timber was busy with birds – gorgeous crimson-breasted shrikes duetted, the male responding with a clipped '*tju*' to the female's whistling challenge; ubiquitous white-crowned sparrow weavers squabbled domestically at woven nests like balls of golden hay. I saw, for the first time on this trip, a party of long-tailed glossy starlings – a species that in the west reaches its southern limit in Kaokoland. A lone hoopoe called forlornly and, inconsolable, reiterated its lament with a piercing poignancy.

In the near distance a young boy grilled his day's catch of small birds he had dropped with his slingshot over a bed of glowing coals. The greater proportion of the tiny morsels would later be sold in Opuwa for cash. The smell of singed feathers conjured up memories of similar hunting exploits in my own boyhood.

Soon after sunset the reluctant witness came silently in from the dark, squatted by the fire and mumbled something to Lucas. Lucas looked at Chris and shook his head – the man still wouldn't talk. Earler, Elias – ever the pragmatist and an unerringly accurate barometer of the local prevailing sentiments – had told me that he fully understood the man's refusal to name names. It had nothing to do with loyalty; what it boiled down to was, how would the man earn money in the future if he put his buyer in gaol?

The young poacher held his head stiffly to one side and gingerly massaged his neck. When asked what was ailing him, he sullenly replied that he had been beaten up by a black constable for refusing to co-operate. The popular term for this type of interrogation is to give the prisoner 'a good hiding', relying for justification on the venerable and useful expression, 'it's all he understands'. Apparently it is difficult to tell whether someone is genuinely ignorant or simply refusing to talk, so when information is not forthcoming, interrogation continues, until the man cracks or the

Above: *Two Himba warrior poachers – the man on the right later joined Garth's auxiliaries*

Below: *The distinctive hairstyles of young Himba girls in Kaokoland*

inquisitor is satisfied he really knows nothing. On this occasion the hiding had meant a few cuffs and slaps but once in a while, in important cases, especially those related to anti-insurgency measures, the prisoner is given a hiding which leads to death.

My trip to Kaokoland coincided with a hearing in the Windhoek High Court that dealt with an August night in Opuwa, in 1980, when a fifty-five year old father of eight, Johannes Kakuva, died while in police custody. The illiterate Herero tribesman had been one of an original group of twenty-five villagers from Okavare, detained for questioning in regard to alleged assistance to Swapo guerillas. According to testimony, a senior ranking officer of the Security Police had the detainees brought to the verandah of his house in Opuwa, where, during the course of the investigation, a substantial number of them were tortured. Their hands had been tied behind their backs, and after they had been blindfolded they were ordered to lie on their stomachs and had been beaten, unremittingly at times. An electric shock apparatus had also been used. Some of the witnesses said that when a question had been put to them, such as: 'Old man, you are from Swapo,' they were not given an opportunity to reply, but beating started immediately and continued.

One of the witnesses recalled how he had heard Kakuva scream, how his voice started to fade and eventually died down until one could no longer hear his whimpering. The witness said he had then had a soft, heavy weight placed on his chest. He had managed to slightly shift his blindfold and saw it was the apparently lifeless body of Kakuva that lay on top of him. One of the guards noticed that he had moved his blindfold and told him, 'If you look again, you'll get killed.' At some stage water was thrown over Kakuva in an attempt to revive him, then the witness on whom Kakuva lay was taken away. He never saw Kakuva again.

The Kakuva case demonstrated all too graphically the deadly predicament many of the peasants living in northern Namibia find themselves in. If Swapo insurgents arrive at their kraals at night, the villagers have to give them food or they will be shot. But when the security forces arrive the next day they are accused of helping Swapo, and are punished accordingly. To an appalling degree, daily tribal life in the north has become a struggle to escape from paralysing fear.

The night we spent camped alongside Opuwa had the macabre quality of a sequence from *Apocalypse Now*. The darkness was pummelled by the throb of heavy rock music coming from the local discotheque that was run, so Chris informed me, by a Portuguese-speaking mulatto from Angola. 'Bloody troublemakers,' he said. 'Had one here with a finger in every shady deal in the district. The police ran him out of town. He didn't like it, complained like hell, but that was about all he could do and he's not here now.'

Suddenly a shot rang out, followed by another. No-one around our fire made any comment, although the firing was coming from town. The music played on, indeed the crack of the guns added a bizarre staccato syncopation. 'Do those shots have any special significance?' I inquired with strained levity. 'Shots are always going off in this town,' Chris answered flippantly. 'Nothing serious. Just the police being sociable – letting Swapo know they're awake and on the job.' A moment later there was a burst of automatic fire. 'What an evil, God-forsaken place this is,' I said, sickened by the spectre of casual, random violence and the desecration of what had once been a lovely, lonely valley. 'You can say that again,' Chris agreed with heartfelt disgust.

In the early hours of the morning, at cock's first crowing, with the sky still bright with stars, a drunken reveller bellowed an unintelligible phrase, perhaps a curse or an obscenity, and repeated himself with savage incoherence. His hoarse, angry cries disturbed a dog that bayed in reply; other dogs joined in, then all the roosters started chorusing. Throughout the night there had been the intermittent rattle of gun fire, and now came an explosion that I imagined to be a mortar shell detonating. I lay on my back, wide awake, listening to the stricken man's rage burn itself out, ebb to a mutter then lapse into silence. I lay without moving till there was light in the sky and it was time to get up.

# 8

# Kaokoland: Westwards

We left Opuwa with a sense of relief and without a backward glance. Garth took the lead, with Chris lagging far enough behind to avoid the pillar of dust that boiled up in our wake. We drove westwards down alluvial valleys bounded by rounded, rolling dolomite hills, feeling pleased with ourselves and content to be back on the road again. Forty kilometres on we arrived at Kaoko Otavi where the strongest fountainhead in Kaokoland – more fecund even than the springs of Sesfontein – pulsates from a rough limestone basin to form a large sedge-lined pool. The water bubbles spasmodically from its source in an action that reminded the Herero cattle-herders of a calf drinking from a cow, when it jerks the udder to make the milk flow. The Hereros call this jerking *tava*, hence the name Otavi, and it is a name that was applied to several springs throughout the Herero's historical grazing lands.

Proximate to the spring, beneath an ancient leadwood, are the ruins of a stone church that was built in 1879 by a party of Thirstland Trekkers, during a sixteen month sojourn in the course of their epic wanderings. They had left their Transvaal farms in the winter of 1874, driven by a nomadic impulse not even they could define: 'The cause of our wanderlust was not clear. Our homes were restful and good. We had no objection to the government of our land, nor to any taxes, nor was there any conflict of religion. But a moving spirit of trek was in our hearts, the cause of which we ourselves could not grasp.'

Trek! – the word cracks like a bullwhip over the heads of a span of oxen. Time and again the Boers had responded to its lure. Perhaps at the heart of its appeal was a subliminal yearning to discover a mystic promised land, or maybe it had simply become a way of life, a need to forever seek out new horizons. Whatever the motivation, the 'spirit of trek' stirred thirteen families to set out in their covered wagons on an odyssey that, for most of them, would involve harrowing hardships and demand heroic endurance.

At the edge of the Botswana thirstland, three of the families turned back. The remainder rested for three months to prepare for what they knew would be an arduous crossing, then plunged on into the burning Kalahari Desert. The trek had divided into three groups, the parties departing at two-day intervals so that not all the wagons would arrive at the waterholes at the same time.

But 'the terrible wastes' that Livingstone had spoken of were worse than the Trek Boer's worst imaginings. Oxen were driven to the limits of their endurance and beyond – many died of thirst while still in harness. On occasions the wagons were temporarily marooned, when the oxen stampeded on smelling distant water. But, helped by Tswana tribesmen, the Trekkers pressed on, and eight months after disappearing into the Great Thirst they emerged exhausted at Rietfontein, on Namibia's eastern boundary.

The good water supply and grazing they found there offered a welcome sanctuary, but the prospect of permanent settlement was thwarted by the paramount chief of the Hereros, Maherero, who feared the Trekkers were the vanguard of a larger immigration that would eventually threaten the tribe's lands. So, two years after arriving in Namibia, the Trekkers were on the move again, this time together with two other parties of Transvaal Boers that had suffered and succeeded in crossing the Kalahari. The wagon train forged northwards, through the Debra Veld to Leeupan, then swung westwards past Etosha Pan and on to the copious spring and abundant hunting grounds at Kaoko Otavi.

Elements of the Trekkers also occupied the springs at Otjitundua and Ombombo, and may have hoped they had found what they were seeking. They hewed building blocks from limestone boulders, and laid irrigation furrows from the springs to fertile gardens. In the surrounding mopane and terminalia woodlands they slew elephants and rhino; kudus provided them with biltong and leather. But rain, the most important ingredient, was in short supply and wholly inadequate to maintain the volume of good grazing required by sedentary herds of cattle. In Kaokoland the Trekkers were confronted by one of the immutable lores of arid lands – to ensure sufficient year-round grazing requires an opportunistic, nomadic existence, a continual moving from the dry or overgrazed to the sprouting or unused. The wild herbivores had, through the millennia, adapted to the rhythms and shifts ordained by erratic rain 'pulses', and the Herero pastoralists had followed suite. But the Trekkers dreamed of verdant pastures that would permit settled habitation, and this Kaokoland could not furnish. Again they harnessed their oxen and, turning their backs on Namibia, they proceeded north to Humpata in Angola, leaving behind their stone dwellings and sixteen graves of those who had died there from fatigue and malaria.

The Hereros that later settled at Kaoko Otavi came by way of Angola, having fled there after the war with Germany. They opened up the irrigation furrows laid down by the Trekkers and reactivated the gardens. That irrigation is still in use today; Elias and I walked down its green-margined course till we came on a shy Himba woman scooping water into a bucket. Elias asked her on my behalf for permission to take photographs – a courtesy Garth had insisted I adhere to, although I worried that signalling my intentions would make the subject overly self-conscious. The woman made no reply to Elias's request but merely looked confused, as if unsure what 'making pictures' actually involved. She called out to a man passing by and asked for his advice. He looked me over and brusquely nodded his assent – the few men I met in Kaoko Otavi were all unfriendly or, at best, coolly polite, and I guessed that they associated me with the conservators who had arrested the headman's nephew for poaching. Having taken several photos and having done so loudly, as I had a motordrive attached, I thanked the woman and started to leave, when she asked Elias in all innocence if I was not going to take a picture. She had evidently never seen a camera before. Certainly she looked the ideal of an unacculturated African, dressed as she was in little more than the customary aprons and smeared from head to foot in ochre-tinted butterfat. Yet I was astonished that she should be unfamiliar with such an omnipresent item of technological paraphernalia, and secretly delighted that she felt neither the need nor the desire to make closer acquaintance.

In the village the women were all Hereros, and their contrast in dress clearly reflected the divergent paths taken by the Himbas and Hereros, who belong to the same nuclear group that entered Namibia three hundred years ago. Those that migrated south in the latter half of the last century came into contact with Europeans, who saw it as their task to instruct the Africans that the road to success lay through as complete an imitation as possible of the European way of life and thought. From the missionaries and colonial officials the Hereros were taught that they were 'barbarians', and that the whites were 'civilised'. One of the most commonly cited proofs of the barbarism of the natives was their abominable nudity – a freedom from shame that was a great source of distress to the missionaries. This moral disapproval eventually persuaded the Herero women to adopt the fully gathered skirt, high tightly-buttoned bodice and leg o' mutton sleeve favoured by the missionaries' wives – a costume that, while undeniably spectacular, is wholly unsuitable when worn in hundred degree temperatures. What the missionaries did not understand is that the lack of clothes is no measure of culture or civilization, and that prior to the advent of the European powers, tribal society had a very elaborate set of laws and customs which tribal members rigidly observed.

One of the village women was running a length of gaudy, floral-patterned material through a hand-powered sewing machine of great antiquity. She sat in a circle of adults and children, who flashed broad smiles and chorused a greeting in answer to Elias's salutation. The women showed none of the resentment so evident in their menfolk, and Elias explained that they regarded the business with the police as none of their affair. One of the mothers amused herself and terrorised the infant in her arms by thrusting it at me – the poor thing, confronted by a bearded white ogre, screamed its head off. When I raised my camera, the mother whirled away with a peal of laughter and hurried the child off to the comfort of its hut.

On the dolomite slopes facing the village, fat-boled baobabs squatted in ostentatious grandeur. The baobab's gigantesque bulk and primitive, otherworldly appearance have given rise to a wealth of African legends, and perhaps just as legendary is the contention by some botanists that the tree attains an age to match its proportions. Although its soft wood defies an accurate count of growth rings, recent work with carbon-dating and the examination of core samples from the stems suggests that there may be annular rings of a sort and that very large specimens – those with a diameter of eight metres – could be 3000 years old, possibly the oldest living thing on earth. An opposing hypothesis proposes that several seeds germinate simultaneously, with the seedlings growing in close proximity until they touch, and being soft and fast growing, fuse into one disproportionately wide stem. Whatever the reality of the baobab's longevity, it is a wondrous piece of natural engineering. Standing at the foot of a heraldic soaring old giant – the grey textured solidity of its exposed roots barely distinguishable from the boulders from which they jutted – one understands why these monumental trees take on a religious aura for the Africans.

From the baobab heights the land spread away below me. The village was set well back from the emerald-necklaced blue-green of the spring, probably a precautionary hold-over from the old days, when elephants and lions regularly visited the pool. During his 1934 Kaokoland expedition to assess the status and distribution of the territory's larger wild mammals, Captain Guy Shortridge found Kaoko Otavi to be 'in constant use by elephants'. He also reported that 'the rhinoceros is the only animal in the Kaokoveld the existence of which is seriously threatened by the natives. Around Kaoko Otavi they systematically hunt them, as they doubtless do elsewhere. Since Kaokoveld rhino visit the same waterholes regularly, they are very easily exterminated. The presence of shooting boxes, with loopholes for rifles, overlooking most of the waterholes indicate that they are relentlessly poached. The survival of the few remaining rhino in the Kaokoveld is entirely due to the shortage of ammunition amongst the natives.'

Rhinos have since not only disappeared from Kaoko Otavi but from all their former ranges in east and central Kaokoland. The slaughter was so thorough that virtually all the game species were wiped out, so I was surprised when, on returning from the baobabs, I discovered fresh elephant droppings. Garth could hardly believe my news and insisted on seeing the evidence for himself, as the comprehensive surveys conducted by Slang Viljoen had shown that elephants no longer occurred at Kaoko Otavi. Although it would not be too difficult to misplace a few elephants in that sweep of hills, especially if you were not expecting to find them there in the first place, the villagers told us that the elephants – several bulls – had in fact only very recently turned up, and Garth surmised they had made the sixty kilometre journey from their sanctuary at Otuzemba. 'They don't have old Werimba to look after them here,' he said, with mixed feeling about the elephant's reappearance in bygone domains, 'and this area has a bad reputation.'

We elected to drive on for another forty-five kilometres to the Hoarusib River before making camp near the river's edge, at a crossing known as Otjiu, where sweet subterranean water seeps to the surface. High, elegant fan palms (*Hyphaene ventricosa*) known locally as makalanis, lined the banks, and between their grey-green fronds hurtled palm swifts in silent pursuit of insects. A steenbok – a momentary flash of bright rufous in the late afternoon sun – skittered from sight into the dense, dark, riverine understorey.

The Hoarusib is Kaokoland's largest seasonal river; it rises near Opuwa and flows westwards across a broad valley between the Steilrand, Tönnesen and Giraffen Mountains before cutting through the escarpment to the sub-desert plains. Less than two decades ago the Hoarusib was Kaokoland's main elephant bastion, but today only its lower reaches are intermittently used by members of the remnant Hoanib population when they move north across the gravel plains separating the two dry river beds.

At dark, the night air cooled quickly and we moved up close to the camp-fire to eat our supper. The flames danced and flickered on the circle of black and white faces,

behind which the black tracery of trees was dimly perceptible against the night blackness of the sky. A pair of jackals keeled to and fro. 'It's a great country,' Chris was saying, 'but from a conservation point of view it's a management nightmare. The logistics of covering such a vast area with my miniscule team defies the imagination. I'll have to give them a thorough basic training then get them established in outposts. Their job will be to familiarise themselves with their areas, mix with the locals and feed information back to me. I'm also going to get horse patrols working. Those hills where we found the elephant carcasses – we can go through that type of terrain far more comprehensively on horseback then ever we could on foot.'

From the seep, blacksmith plovers clinked in alarm. Perhaps the now-silent jackals had come down for a drink. Chris refilled our coffee mugs and went on to develop his ideas, talking with enthusiasm. As on our previous trips together, Chris enjoyed staying up late over the camp-fire each night, debating and drinking coffee. Amongst his contempories, Chris is highly respected for his bushcraft and skill in maintaining a very effective operation in utterly isolated wild places. At a previous station in the desolate central Namib, he had learnt to make do. In lieu of a washing machine he had laundered his clothes in a cement mixer. In an emergency a cheap ballpoint pen with the filler removed substituted for a broken pipe stem. His only companion was a donkey that shared his two-roomed cottage at night. But his idiosyncrasies are only amusing asides to an otherwise hard-working, inventive and wholly dedicated personality who pours everything he has into wildlife conservation. Whenever necessary, which is more often than not, he works himself and his team long hours, seven days a week, contemptuous of the nine-to-five mentality that is creeping in as game management becomes increasingly beaurocratized.

Chris is also popularly regarded as being mildly eccentric, because he spends most of his time alone in the desert. It is supposed that he does not need people, that he is happiest in his own company, but listening to him talk, insisting on a last round of coffee before we turned in, I realised with sudden surprise that he was susceptible to loneliness and valued friends in whom he could confide his hopes and frustrations. Chris is a strong man and to all intents fulfilled, but the harshness of life in the desert can be withering, and I wondered if he did not hunger for a measure of sweetness.

For all that, both Chris and Garth are doing what they believe in and what they do best. They are living the only kind of life that has any meaning for them; it is an old-world existence, almost unheard of these days, which was once described as being 'lonely, poor and great'.

But it is not easy, nor is it glamorous or romantic, as it has often been misrepresented to be. The sinewy, unsentimental, inspired conservators that are getting the job done are the opposite side of the coin to those unsteady escapists, that turn up in game departments and other out-of-the-way places, proclaiming their desire 'to be at one with nature', or similar silly notions. One of the most potent human urges is to start a simpler life in a simpler place, but the reality of coping in the African wilds usually only exacerbates the personal troubles of those fleeing some urban crisis or responsibility.

Day dawned cold and clear, and I woke to find my sleeping bag lightly crusted with frost. An unseen flock of guinea fowl approaching the seep rattled a stuttering warning

Left: *Majestic baobabs on the hill slopes overlooking Kaoko Otavi*

and Garth, abstractedly poking the fire's embers back to life, muttered morosely, 'We should have brought some birdshot along.' I looked at him in astonishment, as much taken aback by the sentiment as I was by his tone. 'Why not?' he snapped, angry and bloody-minded. 'They'll only end up in someone else's stomach otherwise.' Then he sighed wearily. 'All the changes that have taken place, it's bloody depressing. It was preying on my mind when I went to sleep last night, and it was still there when I woke up this morning. You know, the whole atmosphere of coming into this country has changed. The Hoarusib used to be one of Kaokoland's big game strongholds. In 1970 my brother Norman and I walked down this river and saw 86 elephants, two rhinos, a couple of lions and any number of zebra, springbok and gemsbok. Now it's practically all gone, and it happened so quickly.'

Chris drove off first and Garth and I followed, feeling very subdued. A note of apprehension was added to the general air of dejection when, a short way along, we came upon two small craters made by a double land-mine blast that had detonated in the middle of the track, at a point where it turned down to cross the dry Okumutati water course. The incident had taken place a year before, when a Swapo mine-laying squad had 'salted' the road in the expectation of knocking out an army vehicle. To maximize the damage to a troop carrier they knew would be mine-proofed as well as constructed to deflect shrapnel, the insurgents planted a second mine, intending that it should explode directly beneath the vehicle's vulnerable underbelly on being triggered by the blast of the first mine making contact with a front wheel. However things did not work out that way. Instead, the mine was tripped by a government truck coming from the opposite direction, so that the second mine erupted in front of it and though the vehicle was destroyed, no-one was killed.

We were travelling across broad laval plains divided by high ridges and mountain ranges. The stony pediment was bare of grass and virtually treeless except along river courses. The region is less hostile than the deserts farther west, but the arid plain under a cloudless blue sky seemed more oppressive than true desert, as if life had been there and had now vanished. We stopped at the infrequent water points we encountered – unlike Damaraland, in Kaokoland springs are few and far between – to check for spoor, as a way of roughly determining the numbers of wild animals still surviving.

During the drought, the Himbas had resorted to erecting low thorny brush fences around springs to prevent the wild herds competing with livestock for diminishing water supplies. 'To make matters worse,' Garth remarked, 'drought and poaching are inter-related. As the grass cover in the dry west disappeared, the game was forced to move east into populated areas, and concentrated at the few remaining water points where they were easily ambushed. Then again, as the pastoralists' stock began to die they were forced to rely more and more on venison. It was a vicious circle.'

We arrived at the Okonjomba contact spring just as an abbreviated column of silent Himbas crossed the near horizon and came towards us. They strode, single file, in naked silhouette against the white sun-reflecting rocks, with a ribbed yellow pi-dog, as feral-looking as the continent's first domesticated canine, bringing up the rear. The scene was an image, an echo from the past – the hard white light, the bitter country and the wild people, their lean physiques combined with great toughness attesting to the prodigious feats of marching and endurance of which they are capable. One can see in them primitive man, in the age-old equilibrium with an environment in which he has survived in Africa all these centuries.

The married women were turned out in the leather headdress that proclaims their marital status, and were heavily adorned with belts, straps and necklaces. Most wore tightly spiralled copper armlets reaching almost to their elbows, and on their ankles the bulky iron beads obtained in trade from Thwa ironsmiths. (The Thwa – significantly shorter and with more pronounced negroid features – derive from a different stock to the Himbas, although at present very little is known concerning their origins. The aristocratic Himbas disdain most forms of manual labour as being beneath their dignity, a social attitude the Thwa, with their technological skills, exploited on a long-term basis by settling amongst the Himbas, and ultimately adopting their language and customs.)

In the fierce glare of late morning the women glistened dull red from the liberal applications of butterfats pigmented with powdered mineral oxides, which they smear on their bodies. The smell of rancid fat is partially ameliorated by adding to the compound the fragrant gum of the commiphora – the Biblical myrrh – and the ground leaves and stems of aromatic herbs. Elias mentioned that they also permeate their blankets with the smoke of smouldering commiphora branches, the seductive scent acting as an aphrodisiac and ensuring, as he put it, that when the men come to bed the kierie rises quickly.

In sexual matters, Elias assured us, the Himbas are spontaneous and liberated; he particularly endorsed their relaxed attitude towards extramarital sex, which apparently flourishes on the socially accepted premise that what the eye doesn't see the heart doesn't lament. A recent consequence is the high incidence of venereal disease that now plagues the tribe. In an effort to stamp it out, clinics demanded that patients bring in their partners for treatment but, just as often as not, that could not be compiled with, as the other person was someone else's wife.

The prevalence of venereal disease is only one of the major problems currently confronting the handsome, arrogant herdsmen and their independent way of life. Prior to the drought the Himbas and Hereros of Kaokoland were the richest Bantu pastoralists in southern Africa. The introduction of modern, more efficient methods of predator control, the development of numerous artifical water points, and a certain amount of veterinary assistance, enabled the herds to increase to more than 160,000 head of cattle and over 100,000 sheep and goats – an average of twelve head of cattle per person. No Himba can imagine a meaningful existence without cattle; the size of his herd is his symbol of wealth and status; their milk is an important source of food; they are slaughtered and eaten on ceremonial occasions such as birth, name-giving, initiation, marriage and death – without cattle the relevant ceremonies would be virtually impossible to perform. Sacred cattle form a prominent aspect of Himba religion, and there are thirty-six different categories of sacred cattle of which every family must have a prescribed minimum. Their language, which is vocabulary-poor in most areas, contains more than a hundred words for the colours and markings of cattle. Their dependence on cattle is absolute, the tribe's social and economic infrastructure

Overleaf: *The Kunene River – the right-hand bank is Angola, the left Namibia*

revolves around them, and during the drought they lost eighty percent of their herds. In that appalling calamity, respected and wealthy *muhonas* were precipitately reduced to the despised, cattleless *musyona* class; faced with famine and disruption the tribe hardly knew how to respond.

On the last leg of our journey we called in at a relief distribution point for destitute and famished Herero drought victims, that had been established in south-west Kaokoland, at Purros, where a strong spring rises in the bed of the lower Hoarusib River. An air of apathy and hopelessness pervaded the camp; poverty and dependence on charity had leached the proud herdsmen's self-respect and they had become neglectful, dirty and uncaring. Women begged listlessly, hissing 'present, present' while squatting vulture-like in the dust. A naked child stared in numb silence, picking idly at the sores that freckled his thin body. A coronet of flies fed undisturbed on the infected eyes of a baby, asleep in a sling on its mother's back. Overcrowding, flies, mosquitoes, disease and grinding poverty; the families that had come to Purros to collect emergency rations had simply stayed on, and had become reliant on an aid programme funded by private donations that would cease once the drought broke. At that time, the impoverished Hereros would discover (if they did not already know) that Purros, situated as it is in the pro-Namib, is too arid to support permanent settlement, and the future threatens to be as bleak as the past.

The Himba pastoralists, forever drifting with the seasons, have remained isolated in their own customs, rejecting the dubious concept of progress. Now the day of reckoning is at hand. In an increasingly crowded world, their way of life becomes ever more untenable. The stabilisation of Kaokoland's territorial boundaries restricted nomadic movement, and intensified the impact of livestock on an environment they are increasingly out of balance with. High stock densities with limited seasonal movement means heavy grazing pressure is extended well into the growing season. The end result is the eradication of perennial plants and their replacement with annual species, which leads to decreased fodder production, and a considerable reduction in plant cover during the critical period preceding the first rains, with a consequent increased rate of water run-off and soil erosion. Yet for all its erosive potential, the region's rainfall is low, unpredictable and ultimately inadequate to promote rehabilitation once a certain grazing threshold has been exceeded. If the herds of domestic animals build up to their former densities, the legions of scrawny cattle will once again cut the thin soil into dust, an unravelling process that is accelerated by droves of goats scouring the last nourishment from the degraded land. Unless realistic carrying capacities are established the age of the nomadic herdsmen will pass, just as surely as did that of the hunter-gatherer, and the omens are that it will disappear in a blizzard of dust storms as the earth blows away.

We left the Himbas where they had come to rest, beneath a solitary giant camel thorn, staring out across the blasted landscape – both the people and the country motionless and waiting. A short drive brought us to a small spring called Otjitambi that rises in a dry riverbed, flanked by steep cliffs. Our arrival startled a barn owl from its daytime roost, and the bare earth was bisected by the shadow of a dark-phase booted eagle. The water magnetized swirling myriads of drab brown desert birds – grey and rufous-backed finch-larks and lark-like buntings in the main – among which an occasional male red-headed finch appeared as a darting scrap of colour. A sick lark-like bunting, crouching at the pool's edge, shuffled weakly but declined to move off as we approached; it cocked its head to regard us with lustreless eyes, composed and patiently waiting for death.

According to all the evidence, death was a familiar presence at this Kaokoland waterhole – zebra and rhino bones littered the ground. Garth, contemplating the hard testimony to slaughter, said; 'In 1968 a friend of mine saw six rhinos at one time in this valley, but I imagine this,' scuffing a rhino hip bone with his foot, 'was Otjitambi's last.'

Fresh zebra spoor indicated that they at least were still using the spring, but then, to offset that small sign of hope, Elias discovered a natural rock 'hide' with blankets in place that obviously was currently being used by night poachers.

'Why not confiscate the blankets?' I suggested to Chris, but he shook his head. 'If I catch them hunting I'll nail them, let's leave it at that.' His mild but emphatic rejection of my suggestion provided an interesting insight into an aspect of Chris's nature I had for some time suspected but which he is careful to mask behind a hard-bitten, old style bush-type exterior. For all his outward bonhomie, Chris is very much his own man and not easy to know, but I recognised in him his great respect for old Africa which almost certainly extends to an admiration for the hunter. While vigorously prosecuting poachers, he doesn't dislike them. They are his kind of people – straight-forward, unfettered and manly. If they transgressed and were caught they paid the price, but he would not interfere with a way of life that had been there before him.

Lucas had got a fire going and we brewed up a pot of tea, which out here is the national drink. I added a dollop of honey to mine and was immediately besieged by tiny, non-stinging mopane bees in search of sustenance. In the unseasonal winter heat – 'typical coastal reversal', Garth advised, 'probably freezing in the interior with this east wind blowing cross-country, and warming up till it gets here' – common flies were also active, not torpid as they are in the blinding, sledgehammer heat of summer. They zipped from face to face and back again. The grumbling people waved to ward them off – a slap and a near miss, a muttered curse. Long after most other life has gone, the fly, with its affinity for offal and man, will still be with us.

Further west, at Sanitatas spring, the hard plains are of an epic sweep and scale. 'Good cheetah country, this,' Garth remarked, 'but the whites never gave them a chance. Used to run them down in vehicles, then shoot them. One morning I counted six hundred zebra on these prairies, not that they would be able to support those sort of numbers for any length of time – the herds relied on movement, migration and natural rotational grazing.

'Had a close call with lions here, once. I didn't know too much about zebra behaviour in those days. They were making those strange, two-syllabled alarm calls, pricking their ears and all staring in the same direction, but I didn't realise what it meant. I just thought, "Well, while their attention is distracted I'll take them by surprise and see if I can't pot one." It turned out a lioness and I were stalking the same zebras. I stumbled across the rest of the pride lying up in some scrub. Nearly stepped on them. They weren't too pleased to see me – gave me a hell of a fright, I don't mind telling you.'

We saw just three ostriches, sprinting long-legged away to the west. 'Himbas don't eat ostriches,' Garth nodded in their direction. The Land Rover groaned on in the thickening heat, traversing the lonely plains with their whisper of yellow grass. A pale chanting goshawk on a skeletal dead tree shifted uneasily as we passed, but at the last moment decided against taking off. Then we came up with a sizeable flock of ostriches that, strangely, took very little notice of us even though we stopped so I could take photographs. And just beyond them there were more ostriches, a little more wary, pacing parallel to us in an undulating column.

At Otjiha spring we found the tracks of at least fifty zebra that were drinking there. 'Well, that's good news'; Garth was buoyed up by the signs of survival. 'With the present low human population in these parts, the wildlife will have a chance to breed up again – if we can keep the hunters out, that is. This whole area could – will! – become a game reserve. The central escarpment forms a natural eastern boundary; just put checkpoints at the entrances of the tracks that come through the mountains. This country is no good for anything other than seasonal ranching. From an economic point alone, it makes sense to develop it as a park and attract tourist dollars.'

The escarpment ranges are between sixty and ninety kilometres from the coast and comprise a jagged, folded spine of mountains that divide the interior highlands from the low-lying coastal plains. Our road had brought us to the summit of the western edge of the Otjihipa Mountains, where an almost unbroken wall rises steeply up to 1500 metres above the Marienfluss flats. Viewed from up there the Marienfluss spread away, pale lemon plains intersected by dark riverine bush that demarcates drainage lines. The harsh backlight combined with the heat haze to leach colour and erase detail from the cliffs and peaks and great plains, until in the middle distance they became smoothed out, flattened, lacking any perspective. Immediately below was a small Himba village and what looked like a couple sitting outside one of the rude huts, but they remained unmoving and might have been stones.

We made our way carefully down a precipitous and treacherous shale track known as van Zyl's Pass, that clings to arid slopes speckled with peeling commiphoras and poisonous euphorbias. Long-billed larks stood, confident and trusting, on boulders that projected above the brittle bleached grass cover. A flock of pale-winged starlings swept by, the white windows in their wings heliographing an impenetrable message.

At the foot of the pass we came upon the Himba village we had seen from the heights. The inhabitants were all either elderly or children, the young men having left with most of the livestock to seek grazing elsewhere. The adults politely solicited tobacco and food and were gravely appreciative when presented with what mealie meal, sugar and tea we could spare. Garth broke a coil from the plaited ropes of Sesfontein tobacco we carried with us, and it was received with soft handclaps of gratitude. The harsh fibrous tobacco is ground into snuff by the Himbas and, given the choice, they scorn any other brand.

The few cows that had been left behind to provide milk were being summoned by a herdsman blowing low-pitched whistling notes on a gemsbok horn. At the end of the

Above: *Himbas slaughter a sheep by strangulation, to assist its soul to leave the body*

Below: *War wreckage on the Marienfluss Plains in northern Kaokoland*

long, straight, whorled horn was a bulbous resonance-chamber, fashioned from the wax of honeybees. Each horn has its own sound which the animals are attracted to and follow. It was a simple refrain, monotonous yet insistent, overlaid by lowing and bleats; a mournful, harmonious, distinctively Himba cadence that hung in the hot African air.

The name 'Himba' is only about a century old, and was applied to those Tjimba-Hereros who, around 1870, at the height of the Nama cattle raids, fled across the Kunene into Angola where they were forced to beg *himba* – food and living space – from the resident Ngambwe tribe. But the beggars were not destined to remain poor for long. Their fortunes changed dramatically when they joined forces with a resourceful and dynamic man significantly named Vita, or War, who later became known as Oorlog from the Afrikaans translation.

Vita was born in 1863 at Otjimbingwe on the Swakop River; his mother was the sister of the prominent Herero chief Menasse, and his father a Tswana who had left his home in Botswana to serve the explorer Frederick Green. While still a youth, Vita had accompanied his father and Green on an expedition to Angola and there met the Kaokoland refugees, already called the Himba. At the turn of the century the Portuguese colonists conferred a chieftaincy on Vita's father, and supplied him with arms and ammunition in return for his help in suppressing local insurrections. Vita became the executor of these bloody assignments and the Himbas, with an eye to acquiring plunder, placed themselves under his command as a mercenary strike force. Early in 1906, Hereros fleeing the war with Germany made their way to Angola and also opted to join forces with the celebrated warlord.

Various punitive campaigns were undertaken in which the firearms obtained from the Portuguese played a decisive role. During these clashes as many cattle as possible were seized, which Vita divided amongst his followers. But Vita's ambitions led to excesses that even the complacent Portuguese refused to countenance. They accused him of looting and in 1920, with a price on his head, Vita and his band tacitly crossed the Kunene, back into the sparsely populated Kaokoland, driving their purloined cattle before them.

The Herero members of the contingent moved into central and southern Kaokoland, with the Himbas settling in the northern part of the territory, although many Himbas had elected to remain behind in south-western Angola. Vita, consummate leader and astute strategist that he was, successfully transplanted his powerbase to Otjijandjasemo and dominated affairs in Kaokoland until his death in 1937 at the age of seventy-two.

In the interim much had changed in this gaunt land of fierce beauty but, listening to the horn pipe's irresistible music, it seemed that much had remained in place; that, in a sense, history was now. The tribesmen, stoic and close-faced, stood unmoving to watch as we drove into the majestic amphitheatre that is the Marienfluss. The sandy flats, with their haze of grass, are enclosed by great walls of rock: 'It was like another world', wrote the explorer Maudslay Baynes. To the west, the red crags of the Hartmannberge glowed in the afternoon light. An aardwolf crossed our track, took fright and disappeared into a burrow. A moment later its dusty snout reappeared and it fixed us with a black opaque eye, looking bemused and unsure how to treat this ill-smelling apparition.

Again the land stirred as a herd of about twenty springbok, with six lambs among them, cantered unhurriedly away and then stopped to stare back at us. 'They're tame,' Garth worried, 'far too tame. They're liable to get shot trusting cars like that. I've a good mind to chase them around till they learn some sensible caution.' But he didn't.

The seventy kilometre long Marienfluss is bounded in the north by the Kunene River, which we reached at a point where it emerges from the Otjihipa Mountains. The Kunene, which rises in the lush Angolan highlands and goes on to nourish the heart of a desert, is not always as placid as it is here, at Otjinungwa. At Epupa Falls, to the east, the riverbed is slashed by a deep cataract, where the main stream disappears completely into a narrow fissure. Below Epupa, its waters surge through the Baynes and Shamalindi Mountains, bracketed on either side by sheer cliffs that rear three hundred metres straight out of the river. As it continues westwards it flows into the Namib, and near the coast its south bank is dominated by massive sand dunes, before it dissipates into a lagoon at its mouth.

As the Kunene forms the troubled international boundary with Angola we decided, as a precaution, to make camp a few kilometres south of the river itself. We prepared a meal known as the 'hunter's pot', from the heart, liver and kidneys of a sheep we had earlier bought from a Himba herdsman. The Himba had slaughtered the sheep in the orthodox way, suffocating it to death by plugging its nostrils with two fingers and then throttling it. By not shedding blood, the souls of oxen, goats and sheep are freed from the body and sent into eternity. The Himbas also say that by not bleeding a carcass, its meat retains flavour. Once it is dead, they collect blood from the stomach cavity, add it to fat from the intestines together with the juice obtained from boiling some of the meat and drink it as a soup or thicken it into a broth. Elias and Lucas claimed the sheep's head, a highly regarded delicacy, and slowly grilled it over the coals, first singeing the fur off before picking at the sweet meat.

Over the meal, I remembered a story Slang Viljoen had told me about how, in his dealings with the Himbas, there were three things they would not accept: that there was such a thing as an elevator, that there were planes capable of taking three hundred passengers, and that a white man's dog was not necessarily more intelligent than one of theirs. On the last point, Slang assured them that it was only a question of training but when he said that, given time, he could 'talk' to a Himba dog just as easily, they insisted that he choose a puppy from a litter and prove it to them. When Slang eventually presented a suitable trained dog the Himbas were greatly impressed, but their appreciation turned to awe when, on a greeting command, the dog offered its paw. This phenomenon surely transcended the empirical world and the Himbas pronounced the animal to be bewitched.

'It's amazing what dogs are capable of, if given the proper training,' Chris put in. 'For instance, I discovered that terriers make good retrievers. Had one during my high school days and when I went duck poaching through the wetlands he would ride on my shoulder. When I potted a teal or spurwing goose I'd send him to fetch it, and after looking around for a bit he'd always find it and bring it back. I used to give him the head as a reward.'

That night I was laid low by a heavy dose of influenza, which was so severe that at first I thought it might be a recurrent bout of malaria, as the early symptoms can be similar. By the following morning however, in spite of aching joints, a sore throat and streaming eyes and nose, I was reassured to find my condition no worse. Malaria that far from a hospital could have meant serious consequences.

We returned south on a more westerly route than the one that had brought us to the Kunene; past the White Hills and into the featureless gravel plains of the true Namib. Sparse swards of short ephemeral grasses adorned pale flats that stretched away to where distant blue mountains merged into the washed blue sky. At irregular intervals we began sighting small herds of springbok and gemsbok, most of them with a number of young animals present. 'Very encouraging,' Garth murmured, as much to himself as anyone else.

At the Nadas River we found fresh rhino tracks. 'Probably the young bull that the conservators from Möwe Bay reported having seen.' Garth surmised. 'I'd like to take a look at it myself.' And we set off on its trail that zigzagged from one browse bush to another, down a canyon formed of grey and pink ancient granites and pre-Cambrian metamorphic rocks. A pair of grey and yellow klipspingers inspected us from the lip of the krantz in utter amazement, then overcame their curiosity and bounded away as if to spread the bad news of man's arrival. The rhino's spoor plodded on, probably heading for the next dry river, miles away, and our time was running out. Reluctantly Garth turned back, although I was not sorry, as the heat and hard climb had combined with the affects of the 'flu to leave me feeling very poorly.

From the Nadas the track curled eastwards towards Orupembe – the Place Where the Plains Begin – across lonely, broad, dry grass plains broken here and there by salt-encrusted pans, granite outcrops and ridges of dark volcanic rock. Closer to Orupembe the jagged outline of twisted strata rose from the haze, like peaks out of low clouds; the day was overcast with heavy heat. In the old days, this land of stones was characterised by the big mountain zebra, a small family group which we startled as they grazed the tufted grasses on the lower slopes of one of the hills. They made off at once and, unlike plains zebra, their flight impulse did not forsake them until they had gone a long distance. In single file they clambered with marvellous ease up a rough perpendicular path, poised on the summit to turn their big ears and eyes to take us in, then disappeared over the top into another part of the country.

Now that I was at ease, the warmth of the car's cabin acted to massage my ill muscles and soothe my congested head. I had known it to work this way before – a solar cure that probably owes much of its potency to my implicit belief in it. At the same time, the sighting of such promising residual game herds had us all feeling in a very positive frame of mind. Lappet-faced vultures and pied crows flapped from the scant remains of a cheetah-killed springbok, which served to confirm that here in the western desert-lands the prey species were recovering sufficiently to support a small predator population.

Right: *Night watch – a gemsbok bull under a full moon*

Further east, in the vicinity of Orupembe's permanent water, the grass cover dwindled, then gave out. From across the sere landscape came a lone goatherd, a girl of about eleven, ushering her flock from a spring to grazing pastures across a wasteland that, from horizon to horizon, supported not a tree nor a single blade of grass. I watched the forlorn little caravan until it crossed the skyline and seemingly passed off the edge of the world; until all that remained was a wisp of dust hanging in the air, to mark their passage. In their absence, and apart from ourselves, there was, on that endless plain, not another sign of life.